Paper Crafts Workshop

Traditional
Card
Techniques

Traditional
Card
Techniques

Marie Browning

Sterling Publishing Co., Inc.
New York

Prolific Impressions Production Staff:

Editor in Chief: Mickey Baskett
Copy Editor: Phyllis Mueller
Graphics: Dianne Miller, Karen Turpin
Styling: Lenos Key
Photography: Rocket Photography, Visions West Photography
Administration: Jim Baskett

Library of Congress Cataloging-in-Publication Data

Browning, Marie.
    Paper crafts workshop : traditional card techniques / Marie Browning.
        p. cm.
    Includes index.
    ISBN-13: 978-1-4027-3503-5
    ISBN-10: 1-4027-3503-0
1. Greeting cards. 2. Handicraft. I. Title.
TT872.B78 2006
745.594'1--dc22

2006023436

2 4 6 8 10 9 7 5 3 1

Published by Sterling Publishing Co., Inc.
387 Park Avenue South, New York, NY 10016
© 2006 by Prolific Impressions, Inc.
Distributed in Canada by Sterling Publishing
c/o Canadian Manda Group, 165 Dufferin Street,
Toronto, Ontario, Canada M6K 3H6
Distributed in the United Kingdom by GMC Distribution Services,
Castle Place, 166 High Street, Lewes, East Sussex, England BN7 1XU
Distributed in Australia by Capricorn Link (Australia) Pty. Ltd.
P.O. Box 704, Windsor, NSW 2756, Australia

Printed in China
All rights reserved

ISBN-13: 978-1-4027-3503-5
ISBN-10: 1-4027-3503-0

For information about custom editions, special sales, premium and corporate purchases, please contact Sterling Special Sales Department at 800-805-5489 or specialsales@sterlingpub.com.

Acknowledgments

I thank the following manufacturers for their generous contributions of quality products and support in the creation of the projects.

- For metal templates for pressure embossing and piercing and embossing, embossing and piercing mats and tools: American Traditional Designs, Northwood, NH, USA, www.americantraditional.com

- For adhesives for all crafting surfaces, including paper: Beacon Adhesives, Mount Vernon, NY, USA, www.beaconcreates.com

- For parchment crafting tools, parchment papers, window cards, European card-making tools and templates: Ecstasy Crafts, Shannonville, ON, Canada, www.ecstasycrafts.com

- For scissors, art knife, shape cutter, templates, punches: Fiskars, Wausau, WI, USA, www.fiskars.com

- For origami papers and Japanese card paper: Hanko Designs, Alameda, CA, USA, www.hankodesigns.com

- For peel-off stickers, papers: Magenta, Sainte-Julie, PQ, Canada, www.magentastyle.com

- For adhesive and laminating systems: Xyron, Scottsdale, AZ, USA, www.xyron.com

About the Author

Marie Browning is a consummate craft designer who has made a career of designing products, writing books and articles, and teaching and demonstrating. You may have been charmed by her creative acumen but not been aware of the woman behind it – she has designed stencils, stamps, transfers, and a variety of other award-winning product lines for art and craft supply companies. Marie is the author of numerous books on creative living, and her articles and designs have appeared in numerous home decor and crafts magazines.

Marie Browning earned a Fine Arts Diploma from Camosun College and attended the University of Victoria. She is a Certified Professional Demonstrator and a design member of the Crafts and Hobby Association (CHA). Marie also is on an industry trend committee that researches and writes about upcoming trends in the arts and crafts industry. In 2004, she was selected by *Craftrends* (a trade publication) as a Top Influential Industry Designer. She lives, gardens, and crafts on Vancouver Island in Canada. She and her husband Scott have three children: Katelyn, Lena, and Jonathan. Marie can be contacted at www.mariebrowning.com.

Books by Marie Browning, Published by Sterling

Metal Crafting Workshop (2006)

Casting for Crafters (2006)

Paper Mosaics in an Afternoon (2006)

Snazzy Jars: Glorious Gift Ideas (2006)

Jazzy Gift Baskets (2005)

Purse Pizzazz (2005)

More Jazzy Jars (2005)

Totally Cool Polymer Clay for Kids (2005)

Totally Cool Soapmaking for Kids (2004 – re-printed in softcover)

Wonderful Wraps (2003 – re-printed in softcover)

Jazzy Jars (2003 – re-printed in softcover)

Designer Soapmaking (2003 – re-printed in German)

300 Recipes for Soap (2002 – re-printed in softcover and in French)

Crafting with Vellum & Parchment (2001 – re-printed in softcover with the title *New Paper Crafts*)

Melt and Pour Soaps (2000 – re-printed in softcover)

Hand Decorating Paper (2000 – re-printed in softcover)

Memory Gifts (2000 – re-printed in softcover with the title *Family Photocrafts*)

Making Glorious Gifts from your Garden (1999 – re-printed in softcover)

Handcrafted Journals, Albums, Scrapbooks & More (1999 – re-printed in softcover)

Beautiful Handmade Natural Soaps (1998 – re-printed in softcover with the title *Natural Soapmaking*)

Contents

PAGE 49

PAGE 43

PAGE 103

7

Greetings!

Just about everyone enjoys receiving cards, and just about everyone sends them.
A card is a lovely way to acknowledge an occasion (birthday, anniversary, retirement),
express a sentiment (friendship, sympathy, "happy holidays"), or issue an invitation.
A handmade card — a gift of your time, inspiration, and artistry — is a wonderful
way to express a one-of-a-kind greeting. The materials are inexpensive,
and the tools used to make them can be used again and again for card making
and other paper crafting projects.

Over the past few years, amazing card techniques have come to North America from
European card artists — techniques that use paper to showcase the time-honored,
classic skills of intricate cutting, folding, piercing, embossing, and embellishing. I am
grateful for their inspiration. Borrowing techniques from a variety of sources, I have
developed new patterns, new color combinations, and new looks.

This book includes more than 85 card designs and shows you how to accomplish
a variety of paper crafting techniques, including mola cutting, iris folding, tea bag
envelope folding, and spirelli thread wrapping and embroidery. You'll also find
instructions and projects for paper piercing, pressure embossing, and paper punching,
plus a variety of combinations of techniques (tapa, fold and punch) and beautiful ideas
for parchment crafting.

There are sections on the various techniques with step-by-step instructions,
photographs, and diagrams to guide you. A selection of cards showcasing each
technique shows how to use your new skills. So get creative! And start using these
wonderful, fun techniques to make classic cards for all occasions.

Basic Supplies

There are certain basic supplies you will need for all your card-making projects, regardless of the techniques you use to make them. Specialized tools and supplies are discussed in the sections on particular techniques.

Papers

A huge variety of papers for card making is available at craft stores, scrapbooking outlets, art supply stores, and stationery stores. Since this book showcases techniques rather than papers, the cards in this book were made using a small selection of basic papers. These basic papers include text and card weight papers in solid hues, pearl- and metallic-finished paper, and origami paper.

Card Papers

Card weight papers (80 lb. to 100 lb.) are the basic papers used for the base card. The colors and texture variations number in the thousands for different choices available. Some of my favorite textures include a paper with a linen surface and tiny embossed floral design. These specialty papers come from Japan and can be easily substituted for plain card weight papers. You can also find pearl, metallic, and embossed card weight papers. Almost all the designs in the books were created from 8" x 10" sheets; some 12" square sheets were also used.

With card-weight papers, you can cut your own custom card sizes. They hold a sharp crease when folded for a nice, professional-looking finished card. Purchase the best quality paper your budget will allow, as the colors of many economy papers fade quickly, and some less expensive card papers are not heavy enough for techniques such as spirelli thread wrapping or pressure embossing.

You can also buy **blank cards**, already folded, to use as base cards, many with pre-cut windows. They provide a ready-to-go base that can be used for many techniques. Many different colors and window shapes are available.

Text Papers

Text weight papers are lighter and thinner papers – 20 lb. to 40 lb. (20 lb. bond paper is similar in weight to ordinary copier or printer paper). These lighter papers are excellent for layering and creating panels for cards. Text weight papers are a must for techniques such as patchwork punching and mola cutting. You can find both solid colored and a huge variety of printed decorative papers in text weights. Often you'll find papers with similar designs in both text and card weights, making it easy to match and coordinate motifs and colors.

Origami Papers

Origami, the ancient Asian art of paper folding, uses beautiful thin papers in a variety of patterns and solid colors. Their thinness allows you to layer multiple pieces, and they are perfect for folding and cutting techniques. Origami paper is generally found in sheets that are 6" square. Sometimes the sheets can be as large as 10" square or as small as 2" square. It comes in packages of 20 to 50 sheets in a wide variety of colors and patterns. Unbleached and unsized, origami paper is one of the finest archival papers available.

Solid colors typically are packaged in color collections (jewel tones, pastels, bright neons). Most are colored on one side and white on the other; double-sided papers are colored on both sides.

Pictured at left:
1) *Solid colored card and text weight paper;*
2) *Linen textured card paper;*
3) *Embossed floral card paper;*
4) *Pearl paper, card weight;*
5) *Pearl paper, text weight;*
6) *Decorative paper, card weight;*
7) *Decorative paper;*
8) *Metallic paper, card and text weight;*
9) *Parchment paper;*
10) *Colored vellum;*
11) *Patterned vellum;*
12) *Bokashi Origami paper;*
13) *Solid Origami paper;*
14) *Yuzen Chiyogami;*
15) *Metallic Origami paper;*
16) *Patterned Origami paper;*
17) *Window cards*

Origami sheets with shaded or graduated coloring are called *bokashi*. The subtle ranges of color printed on the papers offer interesting effects when folded and punched.

Patterned origami papers are available in a vast assortment of designs, including modern and traditional yuzen (chiyogami) designs, which are the same as those used for making Japanese kimono fabric.

Metallic Papers

Metallic papers are available in both card and text weights and as origami paper. They come in a wide range of colors, textures, and patterns and add shimmer and luster to your card designs.

Adding ground mica to the paper slurry during processing produces pearl papers, which are softly colored, shimmering metallic papers. This paper is especially lovely when pressure embossed or pierced and is available in both text and card weights.

Parchment & Vellum Papers

Real parchment and vellum are paper-like materials created by hand from animal skins. The more accurate terms for the papers we see today might be "imitation vellum" or "imitation parchment" as they are both manufactured from wood or cotton pulp on machines.

Parchment and vellum papers differ in texture, opacity, and weight. Paper manufacturers use a variety of definitions to describe these papers resulting in much confusion. In this book, I use the term "parchment" to describe the translucent heavier papers and the term "vellum" to describe the finer, lighter weight translucent papers. Parchment papers, used for parchment crafting, come in a wide selection of creams, whites, pastels, and rainbow shades. Vellums come in a wide variety of hues and patterns and are excellent for layering. Both vellum and parchment papers are prized for their translucent qualities.

Adhesives & Tools

Different types of adhesives are used on different papers for different effects and techniques. Use the type of adhesive specified in the project instructions for best results.

Glue Sticks

Glue sticks designed for paper are excellent for most paper gluing. They can be used to attach paper panels to cards, for adhering smaller paper embellishments, and for most general gluing jobs. Do not, however, use glue sticks with repositionable glue for card making – they do not hold the papers together well.

A **glue sheet** is nice to use when applying glue to a small piece of paper, and it helps to avoid getting glue on the exposed surface of your card. You can also place a glue sheet on top of the papers and rub down to make sure the paper piece is well adhered. Waxed deli sheets, the 8" x 11" size, are my favorite gluing surface. Find them at warehouse-type grocery stores, or ask at your local deli if you only need a few sheets. Wax paper sheets also work well for glue sheets.

Glue Dots & Glue Lines

Glue dots and glue lines are perfect for attaching heavy embellishments or touching up a loose corner of a paper panel. They come in a wide variety of sizes and thicknesses for both flat and raised effects. For small glue dots, I use a fine piercer to lift and place the glue dot exactly where I need it.

Tape

Double-sided tape is the most used tape in paper crafting. It provides a firm, permanent hold and is thin. Look for double-sided tape dispensers for easy placement of the tape. You can find double-sided tape in different widths on rolls and in full sheets (this is also called mounting adhesive). Because the film covers the entire area, the results are invisible under translucent parchment and vellum. You can use a paper trimmer to custom cut thin strips of double-sided adhesive from sheets of mounting adhesive.

Transparent cellophane tape is used for the iris folding and tea bag folding techniques. Tape can also be used on the back of a card that will be covered with another piece of paper so it does not show. **Do not** substitute the magic disappearing type of tape that is used for wrapping gifts – it does not hold well.

Double-sided foam tape pieces are great for attaching small embellishments and pieces of paper when you want a raised, dimensional effect. They come in a variety of sizes and shapes from 1/2" to 1/8". You can also find foam tape on a roll that you can cut to custom sizes.

Low-tack tape can be used to temporarily affix patterns and templates to papers. Be careful when removing the tape so you don't damage or tear the paper. I prefer 1/4" wide masking tape when working on paper. TIP: You can make your own low tack tape by placing a piece of tape on your clothing – that will "fuzz up" the sticky tape and make it safe to use on paper.

Laminating Systems

No-heat adhesive and laminating systems are machines that can be used to apply instant, high quality adhesive on the entire back of a piece of paper. A laminating system can be used to apply an adhesive whenever a glue stick would be used on a card project and is especially nice for detailed punched pieces, as there are no messy glue marks. Laminating systems can be used for creating your own sticker designs and work well with parchment and vellum in place of double-sided mounting sheets.

You can also use a laminating system to add protective lamination to paper projects and to adhere paper pieces to magnet sheets.

Paper Glues

Paper glues are preferred by many card artists as they provide a very secure hold. New formulas include clear, quick-drying glues in squeeze bottles with narrow tips. Excess glue is easily removed by rubbing gently, making

this glue a good choice for beginner card artists. Nori paste, the preferred glue for delicate origami papers, will not soak through thin papers.

Paper Handling Tools

A good pair of fine-tipped **tweezers** is handy for placing small cutouts and arranging paper pieces before gluing. Alternatively, you can use a **wooden toothpick with a bit of beeswax on the end** for picking up and placing small paper pieces. You can also find **suction tools** that have a tiny suction cup at the end for picking and placing small pieces with ease.

Pictured above – Adhesives: 1) Transparent tape; 2) Glue sticks; 3) double-sided tape; 4) double-sided foam tape; 5) Glue dots; 6) Paper glues; 7) Tweezers; 8) Suction pick-up tool; 9) Low-tack masking tape; 10) Glue sheets

Coloring Materials

Chalks

Chalks add subtle, light coloring to pressure embossed and punched designs – simply rub an applicator onto the chalk, then rub the applicator on the paper. A spray fixative isn't necessary – the "tooth" of the paper holds the color well. To apply chalk to paper through the openings of a metal stencil, use a clean, dry stencil brush.

Chalks with applicator and colored embossed image.

Stencil Brush & Ink Pad

To add a shaded colored edge or an antique effect to a piece of paper, tap a stencil brush on an ink pad, then lightly tap the color on the paper.

Stencil brush, ink pad, and colored paper, with pre-punched spirelli shape.

Gel Pens

Gel pens come in a wide variety of colors and pen widths. The most common nib width, 0.4, is fine for text- and card-weight papers. To trace designs and add lettering to parchment crafted cards, use a gel pen with a 0.7 nib width. White is the traditional color for parchment crafting, but gold or silver can be used for variety. New, wider nib gel pens offer a wet effect (like thermal embossing) on paper; I like these "juicy" gel pens for adding color to peel-off stickers. They also are perfect for coloring metallic papers, slick parchment and vellum, and clear acetate for stained glass effects.

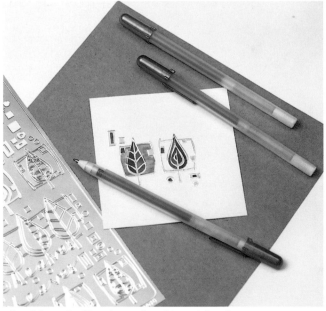

A gold, peel-off sticker colored in with gel pens.

Folding Tools

Paper folding is a simple technique, and clean, crisp folds are important for success in iris folding and tea bag envelope folding projects. Heavier weight papers require scoring before folding for best results; lightweight origami papers, which are designed for folding, do not require a scoring.

Bone Folder

A bone folder is used to score paper for sharp folds. Made from real bone, it can be used to burnish and smooth folds without marking or scratching the paper. An 8" bone folder with a pointed end is a convenient size for general paper crafting. You can also find wooden or plastic folders, but they do not compare with the comfortable feel and quality folds that can be made with a bone folder.

Folding with a Bone Folder:
1. **Position.** Place the paper on a cutting mat. Use the grid lines on the mat to align your fold.
2. **Align.** Place a ruler on top of the paper along the grid line where you want to make a fold.
3. **Score.** Draw the bone folder toward you along the ruler's edge, pressing down to emboss a fold line.
4. **Fold.** Fold the paper along the embossed line.
5. **Burnish.** Use the bone folder to firmly reinforce the fold by rubbing the fold with the flat edge of the bone folder.

Paper Trimmer with Scoring Blade

A paper trimmer with a scoring blade is useful for making long, straight scores for folding. I like having both cutting and scoring blades installed on the trimmer at the same time, with the cutting blade at the top and the scoring at the bottom – that way I don't have to stop and change blades between tasks. TIP: Don't press down too hard with the scoring blade on text weight papers. It can cut through them.

Cutting Tools

Precision cutting is important for successful card making. Here are a few of my favorite cutting tools, along with some tips for using them. Remember to always measure twice and cut once.

Scissors

Most paper cutting is not done with scissors because it is hard to cut a straight edge with them, but scissors will cut both text- and card-weight papers smoothly and easily. Use sharp craft scissors for general cutting and for cutting embellishments such as ribbons and decorative fibers.

Tweezer Cutters

This handy tool, with surgically sharp scissors on the ends of tweezers, is borrowed from the medical field. Use tweezer cutters for trimming small laser-cut pieces or the threads on thread-wrapped and embroidered cards. While not a necessity, they are nice to have.

Decorative Scissors

Decorative scissors come in a variety of designs for adding special edges to cut paper.

Using Decorative Scissors:
1. **Mark.** With a pencil and a ruler, lightly draw a straight line on the back of the paper to use as a cutting guideline. *Option:* Use a template to trace a shape on the back of the paper for a cutting guide.

Continued on next page

Cutting Tools, continued from page 15

2. **Cut.** Cut slowly, matching the motifs on the scissors blades with each stroke to make a continuous decorative cut. Don't cut to the very ends of the scissors points – stop just before the end, realign the motifs, and continue. (This prevents creating a flat space at the end of the cut.)

Paper Trimmer

A paper trimmer with a sliding or rotary blade is a must for cutting perfectly straight edges – I use a paper trimmer with a cutting blade and a scoring blade for creating all my base cards. The cutting blade makes clean, accurate, straight cuts, and the scoring blade marks and scores the paper for folding. (I like having both installed on the paper trimmer at the same time.)

Tools for Cutting Shapes

Shape Cutter: For cutting shapes and windows in cards, I prefer a shape cutter that comes with plastic shape templates – I find I have greater positioning control. The shape cutter also can be used for free hand cutting, and the plastic templates can be used for tracing shapes.

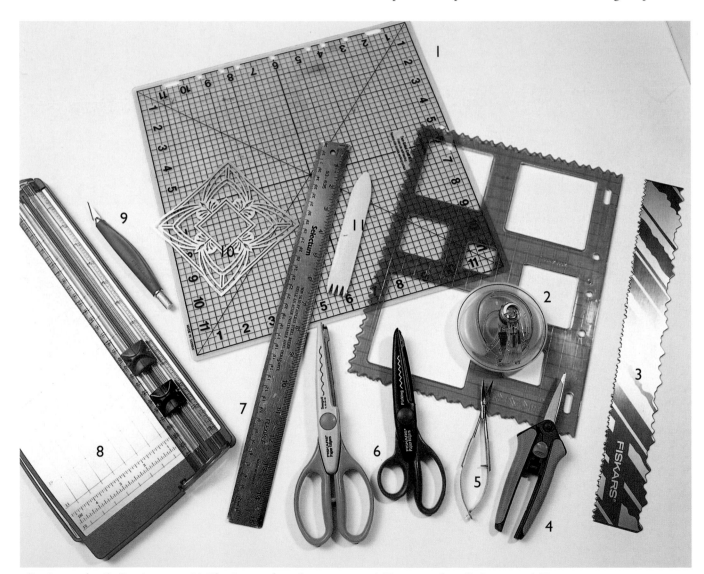

Cutting tools: 1) Cutting mat; 2) Plastic template shape cutter; 3) Tearing ruler; 4) Scissors; 5) Tweezer cutters; 6) Decorative scissors; 7) Metal ruler; 8) Paper trimmer; 9) Art knife; 10) Metal cutting template; 11) Bone folder

Personal Die-cutting Machines: These are used for many scrapbooking techniques. There is even a computer die-cutting system that sits on your desk next to your computer like a printer. *Option:* Check your local scrap-booking store – many shops have a die-cutting machine with a wide variety of shapes available for customer use.

Decorative Edge Rulers

Decorative edge rulers help you create different types of torn-edge designs. Simply place the paper under the ruler, then firmly hold down the ruler while you lift the paper to tear the edge. *Option:* You can also create torn edges without a ruler. Simply dip a clean paintbrush in water and use the tip to outline the section of paper to be torn. Pull the paper carefully to tear along the damp-ened edge.

Art Knife

Even though I use my paper trimmer for many cutting jobs, I still find an art knife an important and essential tool. I prefer a scalpel type knife with a straight #11 blade, but you can also use a swivel blade for intricate cutting. (Ergonomically designed art knives are easier to use.)

Tips for Cutting with an Art Knife:
- **Use a metal ruler** with a cork backing for slip-free cutting. Hold the ruler firmly with your non-cutting hand, and keep your hand on the ruler until you've completed the cut. Keep fingers well back on the ruler and away from the blade to avoid injury.
- **Always cut on a self-healing cutting mat** (preferably one with a 1/4" printed grid). A cutting mat protects your work surface, keeps the blade sharp, and helps to keep the blade on a straight course while cutting. Cutting mats range in size from 9" x 12" to one that will cover an entire tabletop – buy the biggest mat your budget will allow. Use the grid markings on your cutting mat for measuring and positioning the paper. That way, you won't need to mark your paper and your corners will be perfectly square.

Cutting with an art knife.

- **Always use a sharp blade**, and have extra blades handy to keep the knife in top cutting form. A sharp blade is safer than a dull blade, which can slip more easily.
- **Make clean cuts.** You'll make cleaner cuts by exerting a downward pressure on the blade while cutting. Hold the knife like a pen, with your index finger (it's your strongest) on top of the handle. Make sure the blade is held at a constant, low angle to the paper. Make strong, one-motion cuts towards you. If you press too hard, you can drag and rip softer papers.
- **Prevent slipping.** Parchment and vellum are slicker and slip more easily than other papers; taping the paper to the cutting mat can help prevent slipping.

Embellishments

Stickers

Stickers are always a nice addition to card designs. They come in a wide range of sizes and motifs. Use alphabet and word stickers to add a simple saying or sentiment or a decorative sticker to add an image to a card design.

Peel-off Stickers

"Peel-off stickers" is the generic term for the fine metallic stickers from Europe. They differ from regular stickers in that they are made up of delicate lines in bright gold, silver, or copper metallic colors, and they come in a range of sentiments, designs, and motifs. I prefer to use a one-hole piercing tool to lift and place the stickers. The fine lines of the designs can rip and become distorted if not handled properly.

Rhinestones & Sequins

Rhinestones are a fun way to add a little sparkle or "bling" to a card. I really like the peel-and-stick ones that are available in holographic gold and silver. Because the pieces are so small, it's a good idea to use a one-hole piercer to lift and place them. **Hot fix embellishments** use a heated applicator wand to apply pearls, studs, and rhinestones to designs.

Brads & Eyelets

Brads and eyelets can enhance card designs. Use one of the many setting tools available to make holes and set eyelets. Punch or pierce a small hole before installing a brad for easy and exact placement.

Beads

Beads threaded on cords or wire add a nice touch to cards. It's a good idea to have a variety of colors and sizes on hand to add to your designs.

Mizuhiki Cord

Mizuhiki cord (Japanese paper cord), made from the same material as origami paper, is a nice embellishment for cards. It may be wrapped in pearl or metallic paper for added strength and luster.

Lifting a peel-off sticker with a piercer.

Embellishments: 1) Alphabet stickers; 2) Rhinestones with adhesive backing; 3) Sequin stickers; 4) Eyelets, eyelet setting tools; 5) Brads; 6) Peel-off stickers; 7) Card tassels; 8) Mizuhiki cord; 9) Heat applicator wand and hot-fix rhinestones

Mola Cutting

Mola cutting is a paper adaptation of the traditional fabric applique technique from the San Blas Islands near the eastern coast of Panama. The Kuna Indians, who inhabit these islands, developed the distinctive, colorful form of applique that has gained worldwide recognition. A mola has several layers of cloth. Designs are carefully cut in the upper layers to expose underlying layers and colors and then stitched together. Appliques also may be added.

The mola paper cutting technique was developed in Europe and has been adapted for greeting cards. In mola paper cutting, larger openings are cut from the top piece of paper to reveal progressively smaller patterns cut from the successive underlayers. Layering different origami papers, which are easy to cut and lightweight, gives the appearance of richly patterned fabric.

You can use purchased metal templates (sold in stores that sell paper crafting supplies) to cut the geometric shapes; for the card projects in this book, patterns are provided.

Mola Cutting Technique

Photo 1 – The main shape cut from black card-weight paper.

For this easy technique, you will be cutting freehand with an art knife. First, you cut out the main shape from a card-weight piece of paper; after the shape is cut, you tape another piece of paper to the back of the card paper. You then cut openings in the second piece of paper, leaving a small border of color in the openings of the main shape. After that, you keep adding papers and cutting out the shapes, up to five layers. It's unique and dramatic!

Mola Cutting, Step by Step:

1. Place a cutting mat on your work surface. Do all your cutting on the mat.

2. Cut out the main shape from a dark-colored card-weight paper. Photo 1 shows a sample shape cut with a shape cutter and a star template; you can also use a paper pattern or a mola cutting template.

3. Tape a piece of text-weight paper to the back of the cut shape. Cut the text-weight paper with an art knife, following the

Photo 2 – Second paper panel taped behind first panel and cut.

contours and leaving a 1/8" border. Do not worry if your cutting is not perfect – slight imperfections only add to the folk art look.

4. Tape another piece of text weight paper to the back of the card piece. Again, cut out the shapes, leaving another 1/8" border. *Option:* As the design becomes smaller, vary the size or shape of the border (for example, cut it a bit larger).

5. Repeat, adding additional layers of text-weight paper – many or just a few layers, depending on the look you want. Add a layer to the back to finish the design and mount on a blank card.

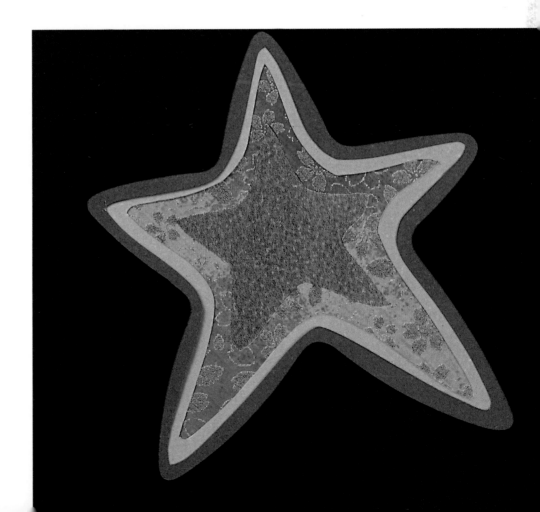

Richelieu Card

This card was made in the Mola cutting tradition using a metal cutting and embossing template referred to as Richelieu. The template allows you to easily cut intricate shapes and add beautiful embossed details. Look for other Mola cutting templates at paper crafting stores.

Finished size: 4-1/4" square

SUPPLIES

Papers:

Base card – Moss green card-weight, 4-1/4" x 8-1/2", folded

Front panel – Green pearl card-weight, 4-1/2" square

Layers for mola cutting – Light green pearl text weight, patterned origami, gold metallic origami

Adhesives:

Low-tack tape

Transparent tape

Double-sided tape

Glue dots

Embellishment:

Brass bird charm

Tools & Other Supplies:

Art knife

Cutting mat

Embossing stylus

Light table

Beeswax

Metal template for cutting and embossing

INSTRUCTIONS

1. Tape the metal template to the front panel card. Place on a light box and emboss the details. See the section on Pressure Embossing for step-by-step instructions.
2. Leaving the template in place, move the panel to the cutting mat. Cut out the larger areas, using an art knife.
3. Layer and cut the origami papers, following the instructions for the Mola Cutting Technique. Use the project photo for design ideas.
4. Tape the finished panel to the front of the card using double-sided tape.
5. Attach the brass charm with small glue dots. ❑

Tapestry & Art Card

Finished Size: 5" x 5-3/4"

SUPPLIES

Papers:

Base card – Black card-weight, pre-made card

Front panel – Rust colored paper, 4" x 5"

Layers of decorative paper for cutting

Art image to fit mini frame

Adhesives:

Double-sided tape

Double-sided foam tape

Embellishments:

1/8" bronze metal brads, 9

3 bronze metal embellishments

Bronze metal mini frame

Tools & Other Supplies:

Art knife

Cutting mat

Light box

INSTRUCTIONS

1. Glue the rust paper panel to the front of card with double-sided tape.
2. Cut one decorative paper panel to the same size as the rust panel. Do not glue yet.
3. From this patterned paper, cut out some of the design so that you will be able to see the rust panel underneath.
4. Use the additional patterned paper to cut out some of the motifs to layer on top of the first decorative paper panel. Use double-sided foam tape to layer the pieces.
5. Attach the finished decorative panel to the rust paper panel with double-sided tape.
6. Glue the art image into the mini frame. Glue the frame to the front of the card.
7. Attach brads at corners and in other areas of panel for decoration.
8. Glue metal embellishments in place using double-sided foam tape. ❏

Island Paradise Card Collection

Pictured on pages 27 and 29

These six cards would make memorable invitations to a Hawaiian luau! Each uses two shades of solid-color paper and a patterned origami paper. To make larger cards, mount the panels on a larger card base.

Finished size: 4" square

SUPPLIES

Papers:

Base card – Light turquoise card weight, 4" x 8", folded

Front panel – Black card weight, 3-3/4" square

Layers for mola cutting – 2 solid color origami papers and 1 patterned origami paper

Adhesives:

Glue stick

Double-sided tape

Glue dots (for the Hawaiian Shirt design)

Embellishments:

3 tiny buttons (for the Hawaiian Shirt design)

Tools & Other Supplies:

Art knife

Cutting mat

Tracing paper

Pencil

INSTRUCTIONS

1. Trace the patterns on tracing paper.
2. Tape the paper pattern to the front panel piece. Cut out the design, cutting through both the pattern and panel piece with the art knife. Remove the pattern.
3. Working one layer at a time, tape the origami paper to the back of the panel piece and cut each layer, following the step-by-step instructions for the Mola Cutting Technique. Use the photos for design and cutting ideas.
4. Tape the finished panel to the card front using double-sided tape.
5. Add any embellishments with glue dots. ❏

Sea Turtle Card

Additional patterns appear on pages 28 & 30.

Patterns for Island Paradise Card Collection

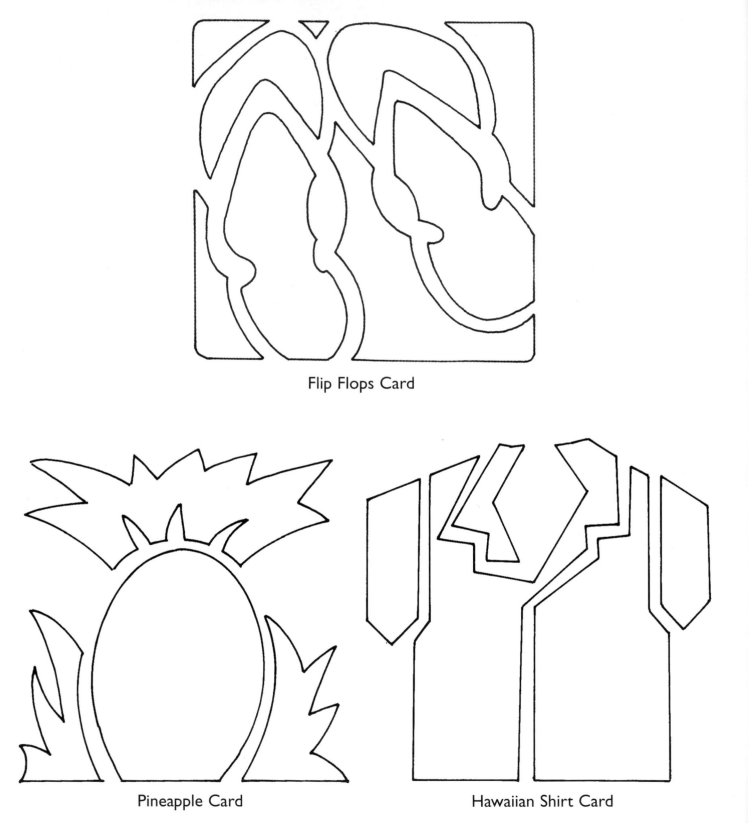

Flip Flops Card

Pineapple Card

Hawaiian Shirt Card

Patterns for Island Paradise Card Collection

Hawaiian Hieroglyphic Card

Hibiscus Card

AFRICAN MASK CARD
COLLECTION

Instructions on page 32

African Mask Card Collection

These simple, colorful card designs use metallic and boldly patterned origami papers.

Finished size: 4-1/4" x 6-1/2"

SUPPLIES

Papers:

Base card – Black card weight, 6-1/2" x 8-1/2", folded

Front panel – Dark blue card weight, 3-1/2" x 5-3/4"

Front decorative panel – Natural handmade paper, 4" x 6-1/2", with torn edges

Layers for mola cutting – Solid gold and copper metallic origami papers, black and gold patterned origami paper

Adhesives:

Glue stick

Double-sided tape

Embellishments:

Beads

Head pin

Black raffia

Tools & Other Supplies:

Art knife

Cutting mat

Tracing paper

Pencil

Round nose pliers

Scissors

Pattern for African Mask card

Additional patterns are found on page 33.

INSTRUCTIONS

1. Trace the patterns on tracing paper.
2. Tape the paper pattern to the front panel piece. Cut out the design, cutting through both the pattern and panel piece with the art knife. Remove the pattern.

Patterns for African Mask Card Collection

Instructions begin on page 32

3. Working one layer at a time, tape the origami paper to the back of the panel piece and cut each layer, following the instructions for the Mola cutting technique. Use the photos for design and cutting ideas.

4. Tape the handmade paper panel to the card front.

5. Tape the Mola-cut panel on the handmade paper panel using double-sided tape.

6. Loop a length of black raffia along the inside fold of the card. Knot on the outside of the fold at the top.

7. Make a beaded dangle by inserting beads on a head pin. Curl the end of the head pin wire with round nose pliers to hold the beads in place.

8. Thread the ends of the black raffia through the curled end of the head pin. Tie to secure. Trim ends of raffia. ❑

Iris Folding

Iris folding is a paper folding technique that originated in The Netherlands. The name is derived from the folded paper design's resemblance to a human eye or the lens of a camera. Traditionally, Dutch paper artists cut paper strips from the insides of patterned envelopes. Today, lightweight patterned paper, such as origami paper, is more commonly used. The finished designs have a lovely feel and depth created by the spiral appearance of the layers of folded paper.

Iris Folding Technique

Iris folding begins with a window or frame – you can cut the window with a shape cutter and template or purchase a precut window card. The folding pattern used is determined by the shape of the window.

The design is constructed from the back of the card and in reverse, with folded strips of paper added from the outside inward to form the iris pattern. The edges, which don't show, are secured with tape on the back of the panel. The complete design is revealed when the folded strips are all in place and you lift the panel.

In this example, the iris folds follow a clockwise pattern. The lines on the pattern indicate where to place the paper strips. The colors indicate the order in which the strips are placed. TIP: I organize my folded paper strips by placing them on colored card paper pieces that coordinate with the pattern colors – this way I don't get mixed up while making the design.

Iris Folding, Step by Step:

1. Place the window of the card over the pattern, right side down, and secure with low tack tape. It's all right if the size of your window is smaller than the pattern; the pattern will work for a variety of sizes.
2. Cut the paper for the iris-folded design into 1" x 3" strips. Fold all the strips in half lengthwise.
3. Take a folded strip of paper and place it on the corresponding color-coded pattern with the folded edge against the pattern line. Begin on the outside edge, working around the border and toward the center. Trim the ends of the strip so they overlap the edges of the window by about 1/2". Secure each end of the strip to the back of the card with small pieces of transparent tape.
4. Select a paper strip of a second color. Affix this in the next color-coded pattern space. Select a strip in a third

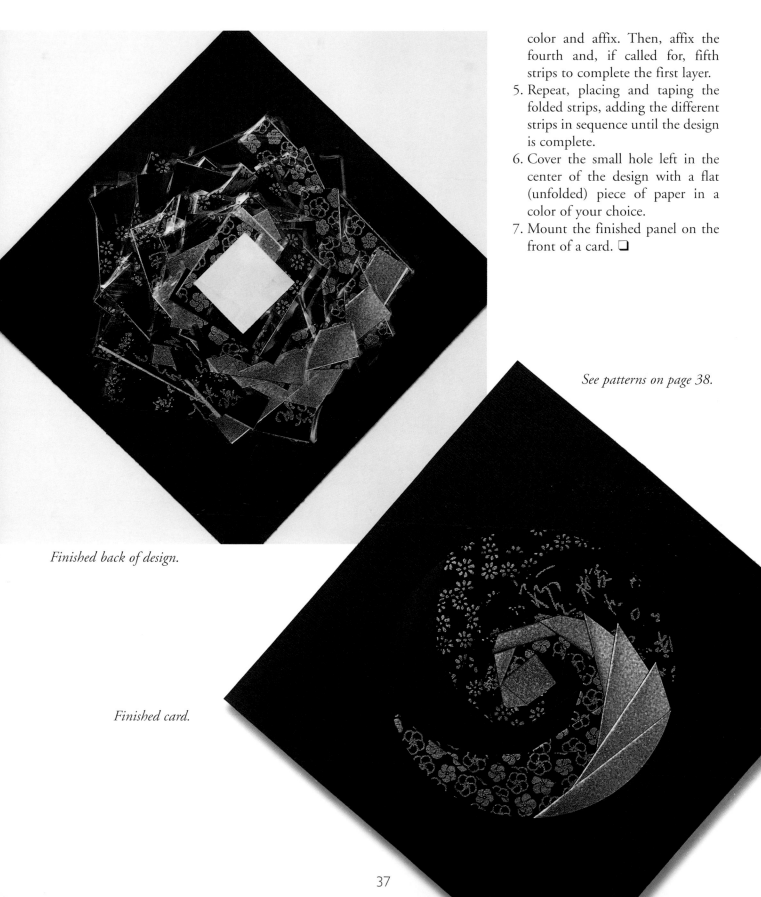

color and affix. Then, affix the fourth and, if called for, fifth strips to complete the first layer.

5. Repeat, placing and taping the folded strips, adding the different strips in sequence until the design is complete.

6. Cover the small hole left in the center of the design with a flat (unfolded) piece of paper in a color of your choice.

7. Mount the finished panel on the front of a card. ❏

See patterns on page 38.

Finished back of design.

Finished card.

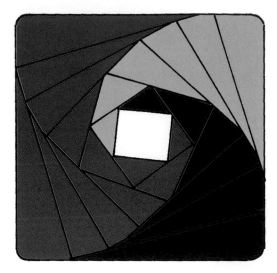

Square Iris
Folding Pattern

Four different
papers are used.

Oval Iris
Folding Pattern

Four different
papers are used.

Circular Iris
Folding Pattern

Five different
papers are used.

Ribbon Circle Card

This card is made with the circular iris pattern, but pieces of ribbon are used instead of folded paper. The ribbon, which is not folded, creates a thick and touchable card design. I chose the ribbons, then the coordinating papers.

Finished size: 4-1/4" square

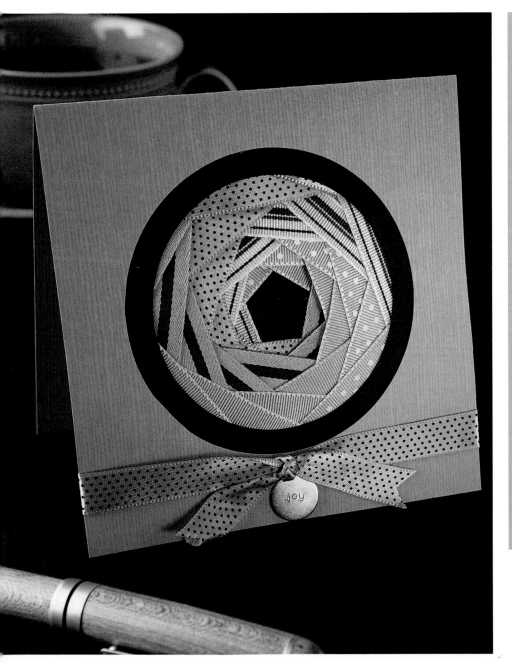

SUPPLIES

Papers:

Base card – Turquoise card weight, 4-1/4" x 8-1/2", folded

Window panel – Turquoise card weight, 4" square

Inside window panel – Dark brown card weight, 4" square

Ribbons:

5 different patterned and plain turquoise and brown ribbons, 3/8" wide

Adhesives:

Low-tack tape

Transparent tape

Double-sided tape

Embellishments:

Additional 1/3 yd. of one ribbon, 3/8" wide

Silver tag charm

Tools:

Scissors

Shape cutter with circle template

Cutting mat

INSTRUCTIONS

1. Using the shape cutter, cut a 2-1/2" circle in the middle of the dark brown panel. Reserve the cutout.

Continued on next page

Ribbon Circle Card, continued from page 39

2. Place the dark brown panel on the round iris folding pattern, right side down, and tape to hold. Using the pattern as a guide, tape the pieces of ribbon into the window, cutting them to the appropriate lengths as you go.

3. Finish the iris by affixing a piece of dark brown paper in the center. (Use the reserved cutout circle from step 1.)

4. Using the shape cutter, cut a 3" circle in the middle of the front panel of the folded card.

5. Tape the finished iris-folded panel on the back side of the front of the card.

6. Cover the back of the iris-folded panel with turquoise paper.

7. Tie the ribbon accent around the front of the card below the iris-folded panel. Glue the silver charm tag at the ribbon knot. ❏

Quill Paper Card

Finished card size: 4-1/4" square

SUPPLIES

Papers:

Base card – Light purple card weight, 4-1/4" x 8-1/2", folded

Front panel – Floral origami, 4-1/8" square

Inside panel – Light purple card weight, 4-1/4" square

Iris folding – Quilling paper strips in shaded pinks and purples

Adhesives:

Low-tack tape

Glue stick

Transparent tape

Double-sided tape

Embellishments:

Purple rhinestone

Peel-off border stickers

Gold decorative fibers

Tools:

Scissors

Shape cutter with square template

Cutting mat

INSTRUCTIONS

1. With the glue stick, mount the floral origami panel on the front of the base card.

2. Using the shape cutter, cut a 2-1/2" square in the center of the base card.

3. Place the window panel on the square iris folding pattern, right side down, and tape to hold. Following the pattern, tape the quilling paper in the window, cutting the paper strips to the right lengths as you go.

4. Finish with a piece of floral origami paper in the center.

5. Glue the inside panel behind the iris panel inside the card.

6. Tie the decorative fibers along the fold.

7. Place the rhinestone at the card center.

8. Position the peel-off stickers to make a border around the window. ❏

Quill Paper Card

This card design uses shaded quilling strips to create the
iris panel. The paper strips are not folded, but they follow
the traditional iris folding pattern. The resulting card is
thin. This is a nice, simple project for beginners.

Sea Life Cards

These bright, cheerful cards showcase the traditional iris folding technique in shaped windows. The windows are cut with shape cutters, a second piece of paper is placed behind the window to cover the opening, and a simple shape (circle, square, or oval) is cut from that second paper piece and filled with iris folding. (Adding a second piece of paper allows you to create an iris folded design in a card window of any shape. Choose a simple shape to coordinate with the window shape.) The pattern you use for folding depends on the shape of the opening you want to fill.

Finished size: 4-1/4" square

SUPPLIES

Papers:

Card base – Bright blue card weight, 4-1/4 x 8-1/2", folded

Decorative layer for border – Lime green text weight, 4" square

Window panel – Medium blue text weight, 3-1/2" square

Inside window panel – Origami paper

   Crab Card – Dark green

   Fish Card – Shaded green/yellow

   Sun Card – Metallic gold

Iris folding paper – Origami paper

   Crab Card – 4 different greens, plain and patterned

   Fish Card – Black, yellow

   Sun Card – 5 different bright colors

Adhesives:

Low-tack tape

Transparent tape

Double-sided tape

Glue dots

Embellishments:

3 plastic novelty buttons with beach or sea motifs, shanks removed

Decorative fibers in coordinating colors

Sequin stickers

Tools:

Shape cutter with sea life templates

Cutting mat

Decorative edge scissors – Wave

INSTRUCTIONS

1. Using the shape cutter and template, cut a shape (fish, sun, or crab) in the medium blue panel, centering the shape.

2. Using double-sided tape, tape the solid colored origami piece inside the shaped window.

3. With the shape cutter, cut a simple shape (an oval for the crab, a square for the fish, a circle for the sun) in the origami panel. Reserve the simple shape – this will be the final, center piece of the design.

4. Cut the origami paper into 1" x 3" strips for iris folding. Fold all the strips in half lengthwise.

5. Place the panel on the corresponding iris folding pattern, right side down, and tape with low-tack tape to hold. Following the pattern, tape the folded paper strips into the window. Finish the center with the reserved simple shape.

6. Using the wave scissors, cut the edges of the lime green panel.

7. Tape the finished iris folded panel on the lime green panel, then on the front of the folded card.

8. Use a glue dot to affix a novelty button on the card. Tie a piece of decorative fiber around the fold at the top of the card.

9. Add sequin stickers as eyes on the crab and fish. ❑

Fancy Folding

These fancy folding projects are made using the technique of taping folded strips of paper in a window panel, but unlike the traditional iris folding patterns, the paper strips aren't placed to create the iris-style spiral effect. Instead, each folding pattern is designed to fit the motif. By varying the paper colors and the patterns, you can create a variety of cards.

Fancy Folding Technique

Step-by-Step:

1. Cut a shaped window from card paper. If you're using a pattern for the shape, use an art knife – cut straight lines using a ruler and cut curved lines free hand. You can also cut windows with a shape cutter and template. (The shape for the Lantern Card, for example, was cut using a shape cutter and oval templates.)

2. Follow the project instructions for cutting the paper pieces from a thin, lightweight paper such as origami paper. Also cut and secure additional paper pieces for the card. (For the Lantern Card, for example, unfolded paper pieces are trimmed and taped over the top and bottom parts of the lantern.)

3. Place the window panel over the folding pattern and secure with low-tack tape.

4. Starting from the outside edges and working in, align the paper strips with the folded edges facing towards the center. Tape in place as shown on the pattern.

Lantern Card. Supplies list and instructions can be found on page 48.

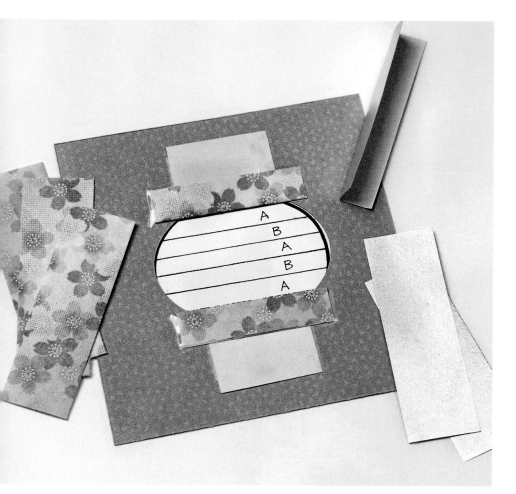

At left: Lantern pattern cut and placed on the folding pattern. The first pieces are taped in place.

Below: Folding finished, front of card without embellishments

5. Place a final strip over the opening and tape to secure.

6. After the design is finished, carefully remove the card from the pattern and turn over to reveal the finished fancy folded design.

7. Add embellishments to accent the design. ❑

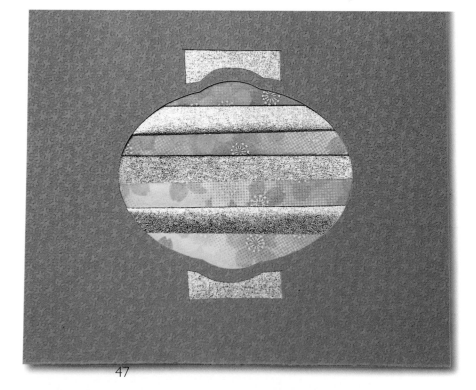

Lantern Card

Pictured on page 46

For this card and the Asian-influenced Kimono Card and Fan Card designs that follow, I used a beautiful floral embossed card stock imported from Japan. It's usually sold alongside fine origami papers in card and paper crafting stores. If you can't locate it, substitute a solid pastel colored card stock.

Finished size: 4-1/4" x 4-1/2"

SUPPLIES

Papers:

Card base – Embossed card weight, 9-1/2" x 4-1/4", folded

Front panel – Corresponding color of card weight, 3-1/2" x 4"

Origami papers – Corresponding solid color and patterned

Adhesives:

Low-tack tape

Double-sided tape

Transparent tape

Paper glue

Small glue dots

Embellishments:

Mizuhiki paper cord

Laser-cut or punched daisies and leaves

Tools:

Shape cutter with circle and oval templates

Cutting mat

Art knife

Ruler

Paper trimmer

INSTRUCTIONS

1. Using the pattern provided, cut out the window from the front panel. Use the art knife, ruler, and cutting mat for cutting straight edges. Cut the curved lines using an oval template. Set aside the oval cutout piece.
2. Use the paper trimmer to cut these strips from origami paper:
   • Pieces A – Five 1" x 3" pieces from a solid color. Fold two pieces in half lengthwise.
   • Pieces B – Four 1" x 3" pieces from a patterned paper. Fold each piece in half lengthwise.
3. Place the window panel over the pattern. Secure with low-tack tape.
4. Starting from the outside edges and working in, align the strips with the folded edges facing towards the center. Tape in place.
5. Center the finished panel on the card front.
6. Add the set-aside oval to the middle of the lantern.
7. Glue a piece of cord to make the lantern handle.
8. Affix the daisies and leaves as shown in the photo, using small glue dots. ❑

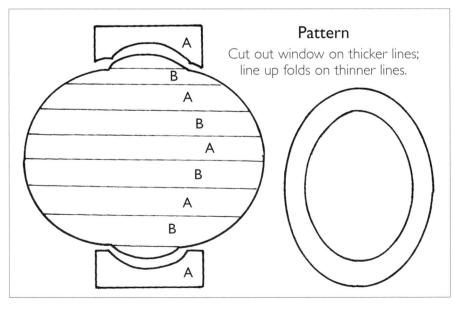

Pattern

Cut out window on thicker lines; line up folds on thinner lines.

Kimono Card

Varying the colors and patterns of the origami paper changes the look of the card.
The cutting and folding pattern appears on page 50.

Finished size: 4-1/2" x 6-1/2"

SUPPLIES

Papers:

Card base – Embossed card weight, 6-1/2" x 9", folded

Front panel – Corresponding color of card weight, 6" x 4"

Origami paper – Corresponding solid color and patterned

Adhesives:

Low-tack tape

Double-sided tape

Transparent tape

Paper glue

Small glue dots

Embellishments::

Mizuhiki paper cord

Sequin sticker

Tools:

Shape cutter with circle and oval templates

Cutting mat

Art knife

Ruler

Paper trimmer

Continued on next page

Kimono Card, continued from page 49

INSTRUCTIONS

1. Using the pattern provided, cut out the shaped window from the front panel using the art knife, ruler, and cutting mat. Use the ruler as a guide on straight edges and cut free hand on the curved lines.

2. Use the paper trimmer to cut these strips from origami paper:
   • Pieces A – Two 2" x 5" pieces from a solid color. Fold each piece in half lengthwise.
   • Pieces B – Two 1" x 5" from a patterned paper. Fold each piece in half lengthwise.
   • Pieces C – Two 1" x 3" pieces from a solid color. Fold each piece in half lengthwise.
   • Piece D – One 1-1/2" x 4-1/2" piece from a patterned paper. Leave unfolded.

3. Place the cut window panel over the pattern and secure with low-tack tape.

4. Starting from the outside edges and working in, align the strips with the folded edges facing the center. Tape in place.

5. Place the final strip (piece D) over the opening and tape to secure.

6. Center the finished panel on the card front.

7. Place four short pieces of cord on the front to make a belt. Glue in place with paper glue.

8. Cut a tiny square of metallic paper and glue in place as shown in the photo.

9. Add a sequin sticker in the center of this square. ❑

Kimono Card Pattern

Cut out window on thicker lines; line up folds on thinner lines.

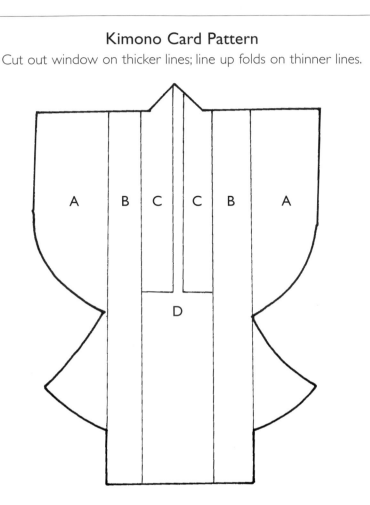

Fan Card Pattern

Cut out window on thicker lines; line up folds on thinner lines.

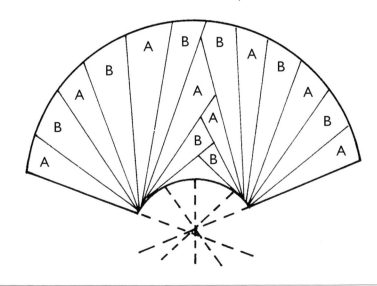

Asian Fan Cards

Varying the colors and patterns of the origami paper changes the look of the card. The cutting and folding pattern appears on page 50.

Finished size: 4-1/4" square

SUPPLIES

Papers:

Card base – Embossed card weight, 8-1/2" x 4-1/4", folded

Front panel – Embossed card weight in corresponding color, 4" diameter circle

Origami paper – Corresponding solid color and patterned

Adhesives:

Low-tack tape

Double-sided tape

Transparent tape

Paper glue

Small glue dots

Embellishments:

Silk ribbon

Peel-off stickers – Border stickers, corner stickers

Optional: Laser cut or punched paper daisy, sequin sticker

Tools:

Cutting mat

Art knife

Ruler

Paper trimmer

Optional: Shape cutter with circle and oval templates

INSTRUCTIONS

1. Using the pattern provided, cut out the shaped window from the front panel. Use the art knife, ruler, and cutting mat for straight edges. *Option:* Cut the fan's curved line using a circle template.
2. Use the paper trimmer to cut these strips from origami paper:
   • Pieces A – Eight pieces, 1" x 3", from a solid color. Fold in half lengthwise.
   • Pieces B – Eight pieces, 1" x 3", from patterned paper. Fold in half lengthwise.
3. Place the window panel over the fan pattern and secure with low-tack tape.
4. Starting at the outside edges and working in, align the strips with folded edges facing the center and tape in place.
5. Center the finished panel on the card front and glue in place.
6. Use peel-off border stickers to create the fan ribs.
7. Use corner stickers to further embellish the card.
8. Cut a 4" piece of silk ribbon. Knot at center. Glue to the fan with a glue dot.
9. *Option:* Add a small daisy and sequin sticker on the ribbon knot. ❏

Tea Bag Folding

Tea bag envelope folding – also known as "miniature kaleidoscopic origami" – was created by a Dutch woman named Tiny Van der Plaas. One day, as the story goes, Tiny needed a birthday card. As she sat thinking, she began to absently fold a tea bag envelope printed with a fruit motif that was on her table. Voila! Tea bag envelope folding was born.

As this new paper craft grew in popularity, tea bag envelopes were replaced by craft papers called "kaleidoscope papers" in a variety of designs and colors, though practitioners of traditional tea bag folding still use tea bag envelopes. You can also use origami papers for this technique.

I use a very simple diamond folded design for the projects in this book. There are many other different types of folds, simple to complex, which can be used to create tea bag envelope folded designs.

Tea Bag Folding Technique

Tea bag envelope folding uses several small identical squares of lightweight paper that are folded the same way. The folded paper pieces are interlocked, laid side by side, or overlapped to make a symmetrical medallion that can be used on a card or as an ornament.

Tea Bag Folding, Step by Step:

CUT:
Using a paper trimmer, cut a thin lightweight paper, such as origami paper, into squares. (The sample uses 1-1/2" squares.)

FOLD:
See Photo 1 and the Diamond Folding Diagrams.
1. Fold each square in half diagonally, crease, and open. (Fig. 1 – solid line)
2. Line up the edges with the center crease and fold. (Fig. 1 – broken lines)
3. Fold the left side of the paper into the center crease from the bottom and the right side from the top. (Fig. 2)
4. Turn over the completed diamond fold. (Fig. 3)

POSITION & GLUE
1. Emboss lines on the base panel from corner to corner and to divide the panel in quarters, using an embossing

Photo 1 – Folding the diamond shapes. First diamond shape is glued in place. **Note:** *the score lines are drawn in so that they would show in the photo.*

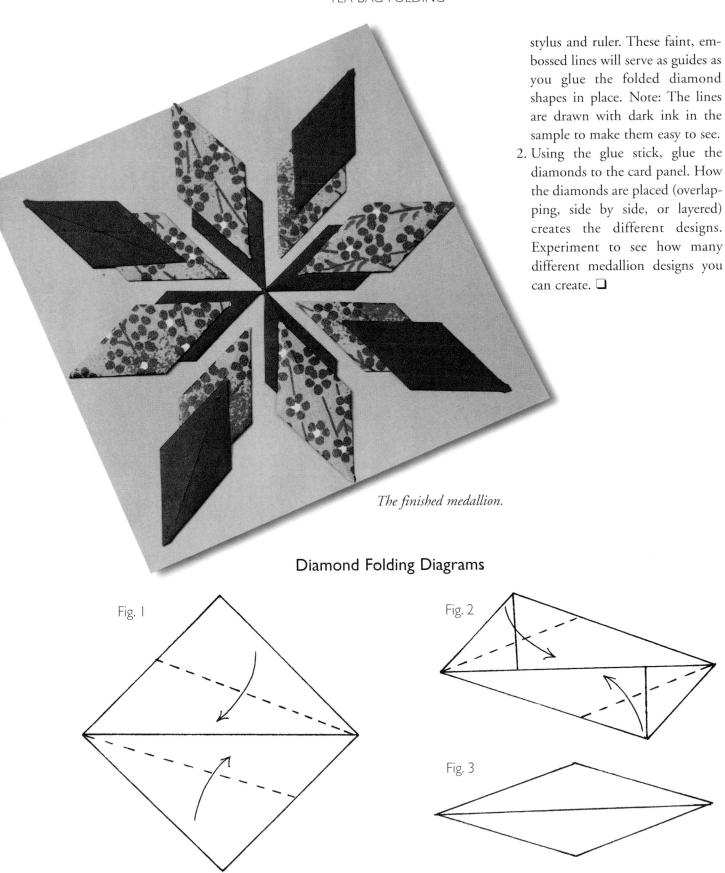

The finished medallion.

stylus and ruler. These faint, embossed lines will serve as guides as you glue the folded diamond shapes in place. Note: The lines are drawn with dark ink in the sample to make them easy to see.

2. Using the glue stick, glue the diamonds to the card panel. How the diamonds are placed (overlapping, side by side, or layered) creates the different designs. Experiment to see how many different medallion designs you can create. ❑

Diamond Folding Diagrams

Fig. I

Fig. 2

Fig. 3

Star Medallion Cards

These medallion cards are all made using simple folded diamond shapes that are arranged in different ways to create the three designs.

Finished size: 5-1/4" x 5-1/2"

SUPPLIES

Papers:

Base card – Card weight, 5-1/4" x 11", folded

Inside panel – Cream colored card weight, 5" square

Origami paper (different colors and patterns for each card)

Rose Card – 3 different coordinating colors to make 12 folded diamonds

Green Card – 4 different coordinating colors to make 16 folded diamonds

Blue Card – 3 different coordinating colors to make 15 folded diamonds

Adhesives:

Glue stick

Double-sided tape

Embellishments:

Gold gel pen

Buttons, charms, or sequin stickers

Tools:

Paper trimmer

Shape cutter and circle template

Embossing stylus

Ruler

INSTRUCTIONS

See "Tea Bag Envelope Folding, Step by Step."

1. Using the paper trimmer, cut the origami paper into 1-1/2" squares.

2. Fold each square into the diamond shape.

3. On the cream panel, emboss lines, using the embossing stylus and ruler, corner to corner and in quarters. (These embossed lines will guide you as you glue the folded shapes.)

4. Using the glue stick, glue the diamonds on the cream card panel:

    Blue Card – overlapping diamonds

    Green Card – side by side

    Rose Card – layered

5. Using a circle template, cut a 4" diameter circle in the front of the base card.

6. Tape the finished medallion panel behind the window with double-sided tape.

7. Add stickers, buttons, charms, or ink to further embellish your design. On the Green Card, a gold gel pen was used to add stitch marks to the folded diamonds, creating a quilted look. ❏

Paper Piercing

Paper piercing – also referred to as paper pricking – is a technique for creating designs made up of tiny holes. Paper piercing is a striking way to add interest to cards, scrapbook pages, and other paper creations. The designs range from the very simple to the grandly ornate and can be done on both the fronts and backs of paper.

The craft of paper piercing is as old as paper itself; it began with the invention of paper in the emperor's court in China, where elaborate pin-pierced designs were used in sacred ceremonies. By 1700, when a greater variety of papers were available, paper piercing had become established as a popular craft. (While in prison, Marie Antoinette is said to have sent a pierced-paper card to a friend.) Paper piercing was a popular parlor craft in the Victorian era – the work included intricate enhanced monograms and romantic verses with piercing, embossing, and cutwork.

Beautiful and ornate paper piercing templates and printed piercing systems are made in Europe, where the craft is popular in card making. European paper piercing, called *ornare,* is described as "the art of needle drawing."

Paper Piercing Supplies

Papers

Card weight pearl paper and parchment paper are my favorite choices for paper piercing. (Text weight paper can be used, but it tears easily if the holes are too close together.) Heavier parchment paper works best for pierced designs.

Piercing Tools

You can buy piercing tools (piercers) with points of different sizes, from very fine to large. Using an assortment of points to make the holes adds variety and interest to pierced designs. Some piercers have two needles of different sizes on one handle, one at each end. These are a favorite of mine as it only takes a flip of the handle to change the point size.

It's easy make your own piercing tools, using ordinary sewing needles glued into a handle – a cork or a 4" length of wooden dowel. If you use a dowel, you can easily construct a two-point piercer. (TIP: Mark one end so you can quickly tell which end has the finer point.) A cork fits nicely in your hand – place your index finger on top for an easily controlled action for piercing. (I find my hand does not tire as quickly when I use a cork-handled piercer.)

Here's how to make your own piercers:
1. Choose a variety of needles, with small to large points, for your piercers. Using wire cutters, cut 1" from the needle point. **Important!** Wear safety goggles and point the end to be cut into a container before cutting – the pieces tend to fly.
2. Take a small nail or wire brad and hammer a 1/4" deep hole into the cork or dowel tip.
3. Use a generous drop of white craft glue to secure the needle tip in the handle. ❏

Mats

A thick, firm **piercing mat** (piercing pad) is needed to support the paper while you pierce your design. You can find excellent piercing mats where parchment crafting supplies are sold or in rubber stamp and scrapbooking outlets. A **mouse pad** or a *1/2" thick foam sheet* (the type used as a sleeping mat when camping) also can be used. An advantage of the foam sheet is that it can be cut to make a mat for piercing larger sheets of paper. (Some card artists recommend using a folded towel as a piercing mat, but I find a towel does not provide sufficient support to avoid creasing the paper.)

Use a **cutting mat, wooden board, or piece of mat board** under the piercing mat to protect your working surface. (This is especially important if you work on the dining room table!)

Wax Lubricant

A white candle stub can be used to lubricate piercing points for drag-free piercing. I find a piece of filtered white beeswax provides the best results. **Do not** use colored wax or candles – the color can be transferred to your design.

Patterns for Pierced Designs

Patterns are included for the pierced designs in this book. I like to offer line designs instead of dotted designs. That way, you're free to use a variety of piercing point sizes and choose the length of the space between piercings for a variety of effects. To use the piercing patterns in this book, simply trace the pattern on tracing paper and photocopy for multiple uses. (You can use a paper piercing pattern about three times before it needs to be replaced.)

You can also pierce printed scrapbook papers or stenciled, pressure embossed, or computer generated images. Simply adding piercing to designs on printed papers can create beautiful results. The piercing can be done around the motifs to accent them, or you can embellish a printed design with pierced lines, swirls, or flourishes. When creating computer generated words as patterns for pierced lettering designs, choose a simple sans serif font and loose character spacing. When piercing, keep the holes close together so the lettering will be easy to read.

Beautiful and intricate metal **piercing templates** are available to create pierced paper designs. To use, tape the template to the back of your paper and pierce through the evenly spaced perforations in the template. You can add a printed image to the blank panel in the middle to finish your panel before mounting on a colored folded card. Some templates come with larger motifs for pressure embossing or cutting that add beautiful dimension to the pierced designs.

To make evenly spaced pierced decorative backgrounds, borders, or shapes, use **graph paper** as a guide. You can also use a piece of **plastic needlepoint canvas** or a piece of 80-mesh **brass screening** to add a pierced pattern to a design.

You can even buy **paper piercing kits**. The pattern is printed on the back of a card panel – you simply follow the design with a piercing tool, trim it with scissors, and mount the panel with double-sided tape to the front of a card. Kits can be found in rubber stamp stores and where parchment crafting supplies are sold.

Pictured above – Piercing Supplies: 1) Protective/Cutting mat; 2) 80 mesh screen; 3) Piercers; 4) Homemade piercers; 5) Plastic canvas; 6) White beeswax; 7) Piercing templates; 8) Piercing mat; 9) Graph paper

Paper Piercing Technique

Paper Piercing, Step by Step:

1. Decide which side of the paper you are going to pierce. Piercing on the right side of the paper makes a clean, smooth pierced hole. (You will, of course, pierce from the front if you're accenting a printed design.) Piercing from the back creates a hole with a tiny embossed rim that catches the light and makes the pattern more interesting. (See photo.)

2. Tape your pattern or template to the one side of the paper panel with low-tack tape. TIP: Make your own low-tack tape by placing a piece of tape on your clothing to fuzz it up – the lint will remove some of the stickiness.

3. On your work surface, place your piercing mat on a protective mat. Place the paper panel on the piercing mat and position the pattern or template on top.

4. Lubricate the piercer by rubbing the point on a piece of white wax.

5. Following the design, push the piercer all the way through the paper and into the mat, then pull back out. Repeat to complete the design. When you are finished, lift one side of the pattern or template and check to see if you missed any of the pattern. If you did, replace the pattern and complete the design. When you're sure you're finished with the pattern, carefully remove it. ❑

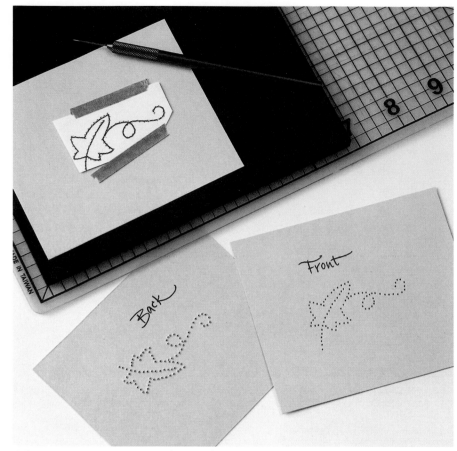

The piercing pattern is taped to card paper. The card is placed atop the piercing mat and then the piercing mat is atop the protective/cutting mat. The examples show piercing from the front and from the back.

Piercing Tips:

- For perfectly formed holes, hold the needle perpendicular to the paper and pierce with a straight up-and-down motion.
- As you pierce, try to achieve a rhythm that will give evenly spaced holes.
- How much space you leave between the holes is your choice. With a fine needle, you can pierce the holes very close together; with larger needles, leave a little more space to avoid creating a perforated line.
- Work methodically – it is very easy to miss holes in the pattern as you work.

Pictured at right: Lavender Sachet Cards. Instructions begin on page 64.

Lavender Sachet Cards

These beautiful and practical pierced sachet cards are made from text weight scrapbook paper and are pierced along the printed designs. You can choose different styles and designs to create sachets to suit any recipient. It's a great little extra to tuck into a gift of clothing or new suitcase – the pierced holes allow the scent of the sachet to perfume the air.

You can use dried lavender buds to fill the sachet or use the Scented Filler Recipe included with instructions.

Finished size: 5-5/8" x 4-7/8"

SUPPLIES

Papers:

Sachet – Text weight scrapbook paper, 8" square

Card base – White card weight, 5-1/2" x 9", scored and folded

Inside panel – Text weight scrapbook paper in a coordinating pattern, 5-1/4" x 4-1/4"

Adhesives:

Low-tack tape

Double-sided tape

Glue stick

Embellishments:

Peel-off stickers – Border strips, label holder

Dried lavender buds or scented filler (Recipe follows.)

Tools & Other Supplies:

Piercing tool with fine and medium points

Piercing mat

Beeswax

Ruler and pencil

Shape cutter with oval template

Cutting mat

Circle template, 1-1/2"

Gel pen in a coordinating color

INSTRUCTIONS

Fold & Pierce:

1. Mark the center of the 8" paper square by drawing light pencil lines from corner to corner. Using a circle template, trace a 1-1/2" circle in the middle of the paper.
2. To create the envelope, fold the side corners to the center, crease them, and unfold. Then fold the top and bottom corners to the inside edge of the circle, crease, and unfold.

3. Pierce a design on the front of the paper in the middle panel, using the pattern printed on the paper as a guide. Use both fine and medium piercing points for variety.

Construct the Sachet:

1. Fold in the side flaps.
2. Apply double-sided tape to the sides of the bottom flap. Make sure to run the tape along the entire edge of the flap to prevent the scented filler from spilling.
3. Fold up the bottom flap.
4. Fill the sachet with dried lavender buds or scented sachet filler.
5. Fold and adhere the remaining (top) flap with double-sided tape.

Decorate:

1. Write a greeting or word on the label sticker with a gel pen.
2. Add the peel-off stickers – border strips and label – to the front of the pierced sachet.
3. Cut a 3-1/2" x 2-1/2" oval window in the middle of the inside panel using the shape cutter and oval template. Glue this panel inside the folded card with a glue stick.
4. With double-sided tape, attach the paper sachet to the front of the card. ❏

Scented Filler Recipe

This wonderful, simple filler will take any scent. It's lightweight and the fragrance lasts a long time. It's not attractive to look at, however, so it's not suitable for display – but it's perfect for these pierced paper sachets. This amount will fill about 10 sachets.

Ingredients

1 cup vermiculite (available from garden centers)

10 to 30 drops fragrance oil – Choose your favorite fragrance or use one of these blends:

Traditional Floral Blend – 15 drops lavender, 15 drops rose

Outdoor Fresh Blend – 10 drops eucalyptus, 20 drops pine

Warm & Exotic Blend – 15 drops vanilla, 15 drops jasmine

Fresh & Stimulating Blend – 10 drops peppermint, 20 drops pink grapefruit

Instructions

1. Mix the oils and vermiculite together in a glass jar. Let sit, covered tightly, for one week.
2. Place in paper sachets. ❏

Pierced Window Cards

These simple piercing patterns can be used with a variety of window shapes and sizes to make cards for holidays or any occasion. For the windows, simply decorate a piece of patterned vellum with letter stickers or draw your own designs on parchment, using the patterns provided on page 68.
Pierced designs show up nicely on metallic card paper whether pierced from the back or front of the card. Mix and match the pierced designs and parchment panels for a wide variety of card designs.

Finished size: 4-1/4" x 5-1/2"

SUPPLIES

Papers:

Card base – Metallic card weight, 5-1/2" x 8-1/2", folded

Panel backing – Solid colored text weight, 4" x 5-1/4"

Window panel – Patterned vellum or illustrated parchment panel to fit opening

Adhesives:

Low-tack tape

Double-sided tape

Tools & Other Supplies:

Piercing tool with fine and medium points

Piercing mat

Beeswax

Shape cutter with square and rectangle nesting templates to make a variety of window sizes

Additional Tools for Illustrated Panels:

Embossing mat

Variety of embossing styluses

Black permanent pen, .03 nib size

Watercolor pencils

BASIC WINDOW CARD INSTRUCTIONS

Cut the Window:

1. Decide the shape and size of the card window. If you're making an illustrated panel for the window, refer to the panel patterns to choose the appropriate size and shape.
2. Using the shape cutter and a template, cut a window in the front of the card.
3. Tape the piercing pattern to the back side of the front of the card. Pierce the design. *Options:* Use a metal piercing template to add lettering *or* print your own lettering pattern on a computer. To pierce from the back, have a copy shop make a mirror-image photocopy of your lettering or trace over the lettering on the back, using a light box or a window.

Make the Panel:

1. Cut a piece of parchment (for an illustrated panel) or patterned vellum (for a word greeting panel) 1/2" larger than the size of the window you chose.
2. Complete the panel, using letter stickers on the patterned vellum or following the Instructions for Illustrated Panels.

Assemble the Card:

1. Tape the panel in the window using double-sided tape.
2. Use double-sided tape to adhere the panel backing piece inside the card behind the pierced panel. (It hides the piercing and window panel edges.) ❑

continued on page 68

Pierced Window Cards, continued from page 66

MAKING ILLUSTRATED PANELS

1. Tape the parchment to the pattern. Trace the design with a colored gel pen or a fine-tip black permanent marker.
2. Working on the front of the panel, color the motifs with watercolor pencils.
3. Place the panel, right side down, on an embossing mat. Emboss the motifs, using the appropriate stylus or styluses.
4. Decorate the panel further by piercing from the front with the panel on a piercing mat or by stippling. To stipple, place the panel on a piece of cardboard and stipple from the back with an embossing wheel. ❑

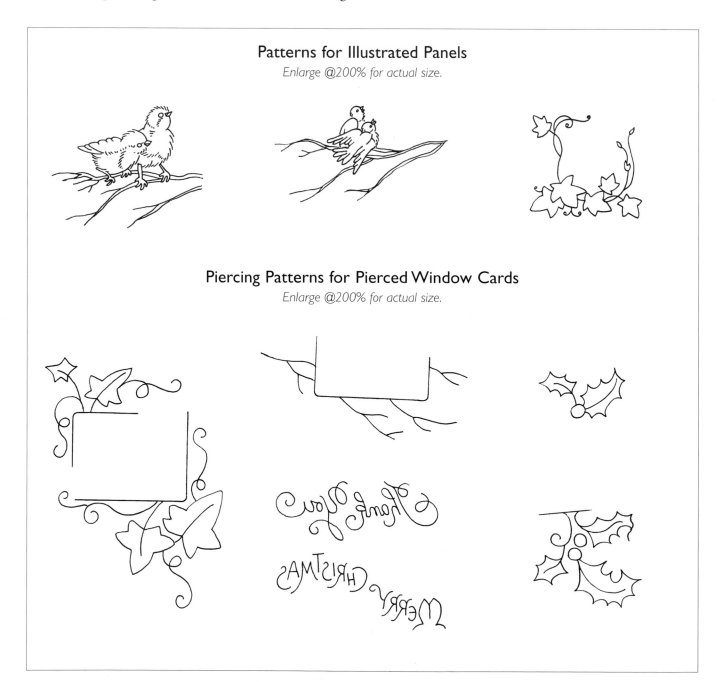

Patterns for Illustrated Panels
Enlarge @200% for actual size.

Piercing Patterns for Pierced Window Cards
Enlarge @200% for actual size.

Pierced Hanging Tags

Piercing is used on vellum to decorate these tags – the addition of light makes them sparkle! They are designed to be attached to shade pulls and hang in front of windows, on lamps, or on ceiling fans. The light shining through the piercing and the colored vellum makes for a stunning display.

Attach them to gift baskets or bottled beverages. Or send them in a greeting card – they're an easy-to-mail gift.

Finished size: 3-1/2" x 5"

SUPPLIES

Papers:

For each tag

Pastel colored card weight, 5" x 7"

Pastel colored parchment, 4" x 6"

Colored vellum sheet

Adhesives:

Double-sided tape

Low-tack tape

Mounting sheet *or* no-heat adhesive laminating system

Embellishments:

Colored Wire

Beads

Eyelet

Tools & Other Supplies:

Piercing tool with fine and medium points

Piercing mat

Beeswax

Shape cutter with tag, circle, and heart nesting templates

Punches – Heart and circle, various sizes

Decorative edge scissors – Seagull, scallop, mini scallop, pinking, mini-pinking

Eyelet setting tool

INSTRUCTIONS

1. Using the shape cutter, cut out a large tag shape from card paper. You will be using the negative portion of this shape. Save the positive tag shape for another project.

2. Affix a 4" x 6" piece of pastel colored parchment in the tag-shaped window using double-sided tape. Place the tape around all the edges of the shape.

3. With decorative scissors, cut around the tag window shape, leaving a border 1/4" to 1/2" wide.

4. Apply an adhesive to the back of a colored vellum sheet, using a full sheet of double-sided tape (mounting sheet). *Option:* Use a no-heat adhesive system.

5. Leave the adhesive backing sheet in place as you cut small shapes from the vellum, using the shape cutter and templates. Use the decorative scissors to cut around the shapes for additional variety. Cut smaller shapes with punches or scissors.

6. Peel and stick the cutout shapes on the parchment tag, layering and over-lapping them to create interesting arrangements.

7. Place the tag on a piercing mat. With fine and medium piercers, pierce around the vellum shapes. Pierce additional details and curlicues to further adorn the design.

8. To finish the tag, set an eyelet at the top. Thread through a 10" piece of colored wire. Thread beads on both pieces of wire. Take one of the wires around and through the last bead to secure. ❏

Pressure Embossing

Embossing alters the surface of a sheet of paper by adding dimension. Pressure embossing (also called "dry embossing") works by impressing a motif in card weight paper. This is achieved by applying pressure with a stylus, tracing a motif over a metal template. The paper retains the image. Pressure embossing produces dramatic effects when combined with piercing or coloring.

Other types of paper embossing include forming paper in a mold during the wet (pulp) stage and thermal embossing. Thermal embossing (also called "wet embossing") involves stamping an image on paper with a rubber stamp, sprinkling it with embossing powder, and heating to melt the powder, creating a raised image.

Pressure Embossing Supplies

Paper

This type of pressure embossing is done on card weight paper using metal templates to create the design. Card weight pearl papers are my favorites, but any card-weight paper (up to 300 lb. watercolor paper) can be pressure embossed. TIP: Lighter colored paper makes it easier to see the design as you work, but papers in darker hues can be used.

Stylus

I prefer a dual-tip embossing stylus with 2 mm and 3 mm metal ball points. While an embossing stylus gives the best results, you can also use the tip of a paint brush handle, a crochet hook, or a knitting needle with a dull point for pressure embossing.

Light Box

A light box provides a light source under the paper and template so you can see the design. Make sure the surface of the light box is big enough to accommodate larger card panels – I like to use a small, portable battery operated light box for basic pressure embossing projects. The light source can also be a window or a glass-topped table with a lamp underneath.

Low-Tack Tape

Use low-tack masking tape to temporarily affix the template to the paper. Be careful when removing the tape so you do not rip the paper.

Beeswax

Without lubrication, an embossing stylus will tend to drag, which can tear the paper. To avoid tears, periodically run the ball tip of the stylus on a piece of white filtered beeswax or a white candle. The wax acts as a lubri-cant so the stylus moves more smoothly across the paper surface as you emboss. **Never** use a colored wax candle – it can impart color permanently on the paper. *Option:* Some card artists rub a piece of wax paper over the back of the paper to make embossing easier.

Metal Templates

There are many different metal template designs available. Look for metal templates in card making, rubber stamp, and scrapbooking stores. Some include piercing and cutting designs along with embossing for making mixed-technique cards. The combination of pressure embossing and piercing makes lovely cards.

Pressure embossing supplies: 1) 1/4" wide low-tack masking tape; 2) Embossing mat: 3) Beeswax; 4) Duo-end embossing stylus; 5) Metal stencils; 6) Light box

Pressure Embossing Technique

Embossing produces a raised design on the front of the card stock. **Always** emboss on the back of the card paper. Note: If the paper is dark-colored, you will not be able to see the design. In those cases, use the blind embossing technique described below.

Basic Embossing, Step by Step:
1. Attach the stencil to the front of the paper using low-tack tape. Make sure lettering appears the right way – not in reverse.
2. Turn over the paper and place on a light source. You should be able to see the template design through the paper. TIP: Turn off the overhead lights so it will be easier to see the design.
3. Outline the design with an embossing stylus. Press the stylus firmly into the edge of the design, touching the edges of the template to create a sharp, defined image. (You don't have to run the stylus over the entire motif area.)
4. Remove the paper from the light source. Check to make sure you haven't missed any areas. When complete, remove the template carefully to reveal the raised design on the front of the card.
5. *Optional Coloring:* If you wish, color the image with chalks. Simply leave the template in place and color the design lightly, using a chalk applicator. When complete, remove the stencil and brush off the excess chalk dust from the embossed image.

Embossing on a light source, using a metal template.

The Blind Embossing Technique:
Use this technique when embossing on dark-colored paper.
1. Tape the stencil to the front of the paper using low-tack masking tape.
2. Turn over the stencil and rub the back with beeswax.
3. Using a large ball stylus, emboss the entire area with back-and-forth strokes to reveal the design. (These marks won't show on the finished front of the paper.)
4. Using the medium stylus, refine the image by embossing each motif. Turn over the paper occasionally to check that you have embossed the entire design. When complete, remove the template to reveal the embossed design.

Mini Card Tags

These cute little tags are perfect to tie on a gift basket or a bottle of wine for a quick presentation. If you can't locate combination piercing and embossing templates, use embossing templates and add freehand piercing. Chalks were used to color the embossed and pierced designs.

Finished size: 2-1/2" square

SUPPLIES

Papers:

Text weight pearl, variety of colors, 2-1/2" x 5" per tag

Card weight white pearl, two 2-1/4" square pieces per tag

Adhesives:

Double-sided tape

Low-tack tape

Embellishments:

Eyelets

Decorative fibers and ribbons in coordinating colors

Tools & Other Supplies:

Stylus

Light box

Beeswax

Piercing tool with fine and medium points

Piercing mat

Shape cutter with circle template

Cutting mat

Piercing and embossing metal templates

Colored chalks and applicators

INSTRUCTIONS

1. Tape the metal template on the front of one white pearl card panel.
2. Emboss the motif.
3. Turn over the card. Apply coloring with chalks.
4. Working from the front, pierce the design on the panel. Remove the template and brush away the excess chalk dust.
5. Fold the 2-1/2" x 5" colored paper piece in half to make a 2-1/2" square card. Cut a 2" circle window in one side of the card.
6. Tape the embossed and pierced panel in the circle window. Tape the colored paper panels together. Tape the remaining white panel to the back for writing a greeting.
7. Set an eyelet in one corner of the tag. Thread the decorative fibers and ribbon though the eyelet. ❏

White-on-White Cards

These elegant cards show off the beauty of embossing and piercing. The pearl paper captures the light for maximum effect. Because these cards are very tactile, they are a perfect choice for blind and low vision recipients. (You can even use piercing techniques to write a greeting in the Braille alphabet – the pattern appears on page 80.)

Starry Sky Card

This card design combines a piercing template and an embossing template.

Finished size: 4" × 5-1/2"

SUPPLIES

Papers:
Card weight pearl paper, 5-1/2" x 8", folded

Adhesives:
Low-tack tape
Double-sided tape

Embellishments:
White and silver card tassel

Tools & Other Supplies:
Stylus
Light box
Beeswax
Piercing tool with fine and medium points
Piercing mat
Piercing template – Village
Embossing template – Star

INSTRUCTIONS

1. Pierce the village design and the outline from the back of the front panel of the folded card.
2. Emboss the stars, using the embossing template.
3. Working from the front of the card, pierce around the embossed stars, using a fine point piercer.
4. Loop and tie the tassel at the fold. ❏

Sparkling Snowflake Card

Finished size: 4" × 6"

SUPPLIES

Papers:
Card weight pearl paper, 6" x 8", folded
Silver card weight metallic paper, 3" square
White card paper, 3-3/4" x 5-3/4"

Adhesives:
Low-tack tape
Double-sided tape

Embellishments:
White and silver card tassel
Stickers – Silver border "Let It Snow", rhinestones

Tools & Other Supplies:
Stylus
Light box
Beeswax
Piercing tool with fine and medium points
Piercing mat
Shape cutter with circle template
Cutting mat
Piercing & embossing templates – Snowflake, star

INSTRUCTIONS

1. Use a shape cutter and circle template to cut a 2" window from the front panel of the pearl paper card.
2. Emboss and pierce the snowflakes on the front of the card. **Note:** I used both piercing and embossing templates, but you could use embossing templates and add the piercing freehand.

continued on page 80

*White on White Cards,
continued from page 78*

3. Emboss the stars on the front of the card. Pierce from the front of the card with a fine point piercer around the embossed stars.

4. Pierce a border around the circle window.

5. Emboss a single snowflake on the silver metallic card paper. Tape in the window.

6. *Option:* Emboss a message in Braille from the back along the bottom of the white card paper panel.

7. Tape the white card paper inside the card as an inside panel.

8. Affix the silver border stickers around the edge of the card. Add rhinestone stickers to the silver snowflake for extra sparkle. ❏

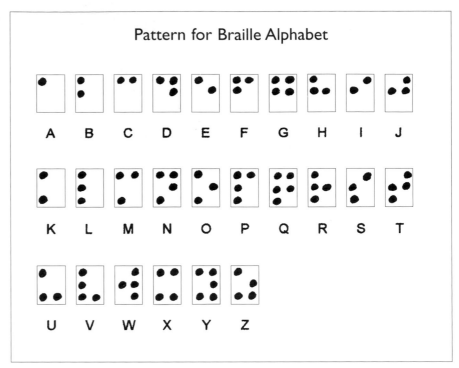

Pattern for Braille Alphabet

A B C D E F G H I J

K L M N O P Q R S T

U V W X Y Z

Square Silver & White Card

Finished size: 5" square

SUPPLIES

Papers:

Card weight pearl paper (Cut the panel 1/2" larger than the template.)

Silver text weight metallic paper, 5" square

White card paper, 5" x 10", folded

Adhesives:

Low-tack tape

Double-sided tape

Embellishments:

White and silver card tassel

Tools & Other Supplies:

Stylus

Light box

Beeswax

Piercing tool with fine and medium points

Piercing mat

Piercing and embossing metal templates

INSTRUCTIONS

1. Place the embossing template on the front of the pearl paper panel. Emboss the design.

2. Tape the piercing template to the back of the panel. Working from the back, pierce the design.

3. Mount the silver paper on the white card with double-sided tape.

4. Mount the pierced and embossed panel at the center of the silver panel. Loop and tie the tassel at the fold. ❏

Square Silver & White Card

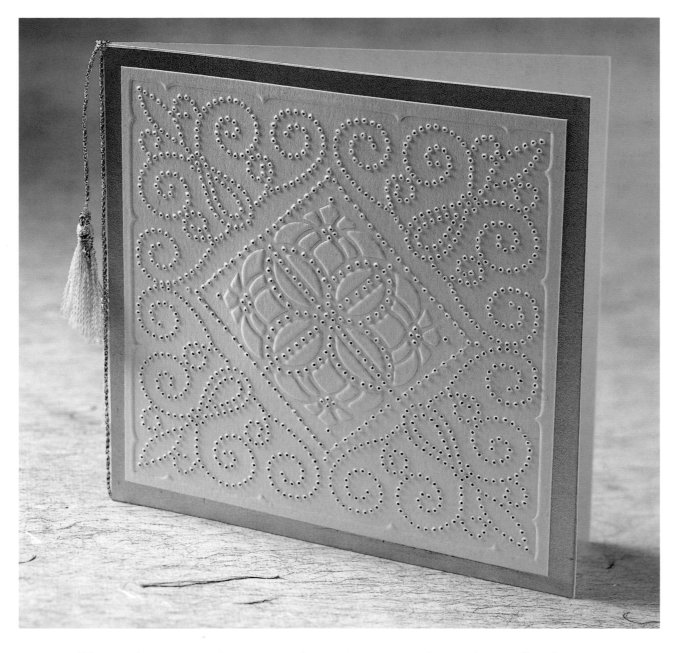

This card was created using a card size piercing template and a small embossing template for the center motif. The design is pierced from the back, so the pierced design captures light and creates shadows on the card.

Parchment Crafting

Parchment crafting dates from the 14th century when piercing, embossing, painting, and gilding were done on pieces of animal parchment. The work was done by nuns; biblical scenes and saints were prominent themes. Parchment crafting spread to the New World in the 16th century and became popular in South America.

In the Victorian era, parchment crafting themes became more romantic, introducing florals, cherubs, portraits, and machine embossing. Most of the borders, perforations, and cuts were also done by machine at this time. The craft of handmade parchment cards was continuing in South America, especially for young girls at their first communion.

The tremendous popularity of parchment crafting today is due largely to the efforts of one woman, Martha Ospina, who brought the craft to The Netherlands when she moved there from her native Colombia in 1987. She began teaching parchment crafting to meet people and learn the Dutch language. *Pergamano* is the trade name of the Colombian method of parchment crafting that Ospina helped to develop. In Puerto Rico, parchment crafting is known as *tarjeteria pergaminada*, which translates "the art of making greeting cards using parchment paper."

This section includes parchment crafting basics – cutting, pressure embossing, coloring, and piercing. The techniques are combined to create beautiful lace-like cards. You'll find patterns and kits for more elaborate parchment crafting designs in rubber stamp and paper crafting stores.

If you are lucky enough to have received a handmade parchment crafted card, cherish it – making it required a great deal of patience, time, and ability.

Parchment Crafting Supplies

Tracing Materials

Because parchment paper is translucent, it is easy to trace a pattern on parchment with a pen before embossing. To trace designs and add lettering to parchment crafted cards, use a gel pen with a 0.7 nib width. White is the traditional color for parchment crafting, but gold and silver also look nice. Permanent black markers are also used for tracing designs on parchment. Use the .03 nib size for the best results.

A piece of graph paper is a useful pattern for creating a field of embossed dots on a parchment panel.

Watercolor Pencils

Watercolor pencils are my favorite method for adding color to parchment crafted cards. The softness of the pencils makes it easy to apply a shaded coloring to the back of a traced design. *Option:* For deeper color, dip a paintbrush in clean water, remove the excess, and lightly shade the design by moistening the color and blending. **Do not** use a brush full of water – the excess moisture will warp the parchment.

Parchment Embossing Tools

Parchment embossing is done free hand (without a template) on the back of parchment paper within a traced design. Embossing breaks and stretches the paper fibers and turns the parchment white. For pressure embossing on parchment, you need a very soft surface, such as an embossing mat or a computer mouse pad.

This photo shows parchment crafting embossing tools and the effects they make.
Top left: A design traced and colored in with white gel pen.
Top right: Design embossed with a spoon-shaped embosser.
Bottom left: Medium embossers used to add more dimension.
Bottom right: An embossing wheel used to add stippled design detail.

Parchment crafting embossing tools range from very fine ball points to broad shading tools to specialty embossing tools – each gives a different effect. For the projects in this book, a few basic embossing tools are used. **Small and medium embossing ball tips** (2 mm and 3 mm) on an embossing stylus are used to create embossed lines and small embossed dots. They are also used for embossing small areas of the design.

A **large embossing ball tip stylus** (6 mm) or an **embossing spoon** is used for embossing large areas of the design and to create a soft, graduated shaded effect. To use a spoon-shaped embosser, place the tip of the tool towards the traced outline of the design. Emboss with the pressure at the tip to create the shaded effect. Turn the parchment as you work so the tool is always in the proper position in relation to the outline.

Use **embossing wheels** to create stippled line designs on parchment – you can find a variety of sizes for different effects, or you can use a sewing tracing wheel. To use an embossing wheel, place the parchment on a piece of cardboard and work from the back of the paper. **Do not** use the embossing wheel on an embossing mat – if you do, the paper will rip.

Lubricant

Use a piece of white beeswax, a white candle, or wax paper to lightly rub the surface of the parchment before embossing. Lubrication makes your embossing smooth and drag-free. **Do not** use colored wax.

Parchment Piercing Tools

For beautiful piercing on parchment, use parchment craft piercers, which have very fine points. You cannot reproduce the effects of these tools with homemade ones.

A **one-hole piercer** is a very fine piercing tool. A **two-hole piercer** makes piercing go twice as fast. It makes evenly spaced holes and can be used to punch a continuous line around a motif (like a perforation) that can be punched out to create a lace edge. A **three-hole piercer** makes a nice triangle design and works well for the pierce-and-wiggle technique. (Pierce-and-wiggle is exactly what it says – you simply pierce the paper, then gently wiggle the tool to enlarge the holes.) You can also use a **five-hole piercer** for the pierce-and-wiggle technique.

Pictured at right: Parchment samples showing various designs using embossers, piercers, and embossing wheel.

Parchment Piercers & Their Effects – from top to bottom: Single-hole piercer, Two-hole piercer, Three-hole piercer, Five-hole piercer

Parchment Crafting Technique

Parchment Crafting, Step by Step:

TRACE:

Tape the parchment paper over the pattern. Trace the design using a white gel pen or a black marker. The side with the markings is now the front of the parchment. Remove the pattern.

COLOR:

If you want to add color to your design, do it now. Work on a hard, smooth surface on either the front or back side of the parchment.

EMBOSS:

1. Place the parchment paper, front side down, on an embossing mat. You will be embossing on the back of the parchment. Rub a little beeswax on the back of the parchment to make the embossing easier.

2. Use a large embossing tool to emboss large areas. Start with a light pressure to gently stretch the paper – it will turn white. Apply a little more pressure to achieve an even, white area. Do not apply too much pressure – you could break through the parchment. TIP: Use a white watercolor pencil to shade the design before embossing to avoid tool marks that beginners experience while learning this technique.

3. Use a small ball tip embossing stylus to emboss smaller areas and to add dots to the design.

4. Place the parchment panel face down on a piece of cardboard. Use an embossing wheel to emboss the stippled lines of the design.

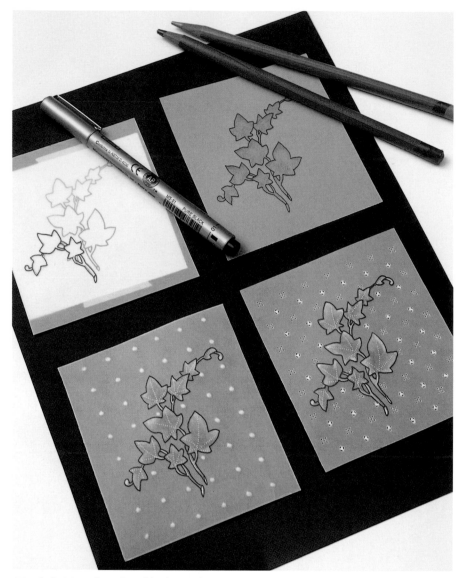

Top left: Traced with a black marker.
Top right: Colored with watercolor pencils.
Bottom left: Embossed with large and medium ball embossers.
Bottom right: Pierced finished panel.

PIERCE:

After the embossing is complete, add piercing to the design on the front of the parchment. Use a piece of 80 mesh brass as a piercing guide or emboss and pierce different design fields using a piece of graph paper as a guide.

Parchamoré

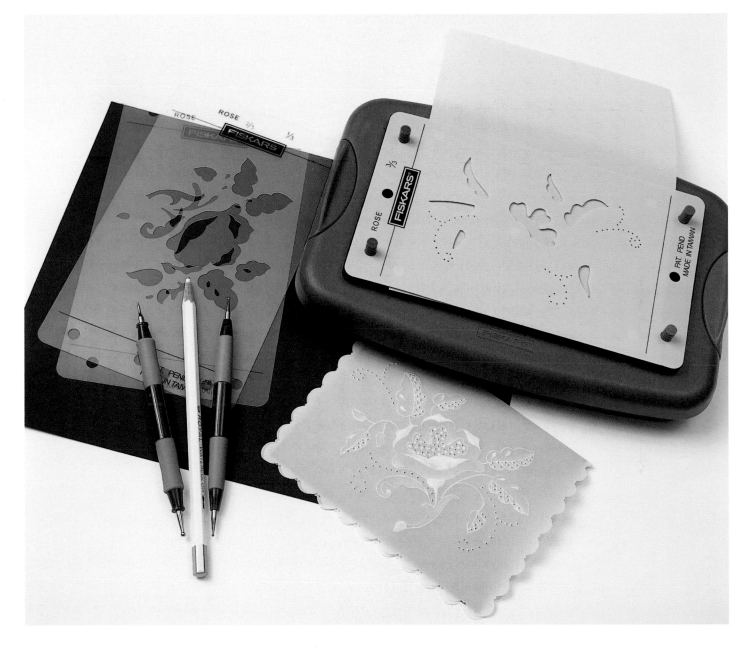

Parchamoré is a beginner's form of parchment crafting that is done with a series of templates on an embossing system. It's a perfect introduction into parchment crafting. The Parchamore system and a finished card is pictured in the photo above.

Victorian-Style Cards

These cards, designed in the Victorian style, have interchangeable motifs for a range of design possibilities that can be customized to suit the recipient. Using the patterns provided, you can add a scene or a sentiment to the center panel, and emboss and pierce an intricate background or keep it simple. The procedure is the same for each card. In the manner of the Victorians, I have included the meaning of each floral motif to add to the inside of the card.

SUPPLIES

Papers:
Plain parchment (type used in parchment crafting)
Rainbow parchment
Antique white card weight

Adhesives:
Double-sided tape

Embellishments:
Peel-off stickers
Brads

Tools & Other Supplies:
Corner punches or circle border punches
Sepia brown stamp pad and stencil brush
Shape cutter with square, rectangle, or circle templates
Cutting mat
Fine-tip permanent pen or marker
Watercolor pencils
Embossers – Medium, spoon-shaped
Embossing mat
Embossing wheel
Piercing tools – one-, three-, and five-hole
Piercing mat
Graph paper and/or brass screening
Paint brush

INSTRUCTIONS

Parchment Panel:
The patterns and motifs are interchangeable.

1. Choose a floral motif (ivy, rose, violet, lily-of-the-valley). Working on a smooth, hard surface, trace the design with the black marker on the front of the parchment paper.
2. Trace the antique paper (window) motif, placing it so the floral motif is on the left. As you trace the paper motif, **don't** draw over the floral design – the paper motif should look as if it is behind the floral design.
3. Add a butterfly, snail, or bee, choosing one of the critter motifs.
4. Trace a country scene or a sentiment inside the paper (window) motif. Again, be sure to not trace over the floral design.
5. Color the floral design, paper motif, and critter with watercolor pencils, working on the back of the parchment on a smooth, hard surface. Smooth and mix the pencil colors with a damp, clean paintbrush.
6. Working from the back side on an embossing mat, emboss the design. (The colored areas will lighten or become white when embossed.) Use the spoon embosser for large areas (leaves and flowers, trees in the country scenes, the flipped up edges of the paper motif). Emboss the lily-of-the-valley flower buds fully to make them white.
7. Use the medium embosser for finer details (critters, centers of the violets, highlights in the trees, bushes, water in the country scenes).
8. Working on the back of the parchment on a piece of cardboard, stipple the veins of the leaves with the embossing wheel.
9. Choose a background design. You can simply pierce the entire area through a brass mesh or create an embossed and pierced background using graph paper as a guide. **Always** emboss from the back on an embossing pad and pierce from the front on a piercing pad.

Card Assembly:
1. Decide on the shape and size for your finished card. Make a folded card from antique white card paper.

Continued on page 90

Victorian-Style Cards, continued from page 88

2. Cut a panel from antique white card paper the same size as the folded card. Cut a window in this panel, using a shape cutter and template.

3. Decorate the window panel with corner punches or a border punch. To antique the window panel, brush sepia ink on the edges with a stencil brush.

4. Tape the parchment crafted panel in the window panel. Cut a piece of rainbow parchment as a backing. *Option:* Use a piece of dark colored text paper as a backing. Try several colors to see which one looks best.

5. Tape the finished panel to the front of the folded card.

6. Add embellishments such as brads or peel-off stickers. ❑

Patterns for Victorian-Style Cards

Rose

Ivy

Violet

Lily-of-the-Valley

Patterns for Victorian-Style Cards

Antique Paper Motif

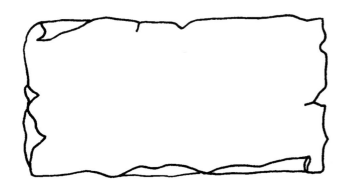

The Language of Flowers & Herbs

Throughout the ages, symbolic meanings that originated from folk legends and sacred traditions have been assigned to various plants. Medieval and renaissance paintings often featured bouquets of flowers that conveyed symbolism. In Victorian times, friends and lovers used the meanings of flowers to send a special message in the form of a tussie-mussie or a pressed flower tucked in a card or gift. Here are some examples:

Ivy – Friendship and eternity, marriage

Violet – Humility, faithfulness
Blue violets – "I'll always be true"
White violets – "Let's take a chance on happiness"

Rose – Happy love
Red rose – Love
White rose – "I am worthy of you"
Pink rose – Friendship

Lily-of-the-Valley – Return of happiness, sweetness

Lace Floral Cards

These simple, dainty cards are made using the same floral patterns as the Victorian-Style Cards that appear on pages 90 and 91. The versatile floral designs are traced in white ink, using a white gel pen. These cards are a perfect first project for parchment crafting beginners.

Finished size: 4-1/4" square

SUPPLIES

Papers:

Card base – Muted blue card weight, 8-1/2" x 4-1/4", folded

Window panel – Plain parchment paper (the type used in parchment crafting), 4" square

Frame – Blue or light purple pearl paper, text weight, 4" square

Adhesives:

Double-sided tape

Embellishments:

Silver and white card tassels

Tools & Other Supplies:

Corner cut-and-emboss punches

Shape cutter with square template

Circle template

Cutting mat

White gel pen

Watercolor pencil – Purple or dark blue

Embossers – Medium, spoon-shaped

Embossing mat

Embossing wheel

One-hole piercing tool

Piercing mat

Graph paper

INSTRUCTIONS

Parchment Panel:

1. Choose a floral design. Working on a smooth, hard surface, trace the design on the front of the parchment paper with a white gel pen.
2. Using a circle template, trace a circle around the floral design. Be sure you don't draw over the lines of the floral design.
3. Add a butterfly, snail, or bee to the design, using one of the critter motif patterns. Place the critter inside or outside the circle.
4. Working on a smooth, hard surface on the back of the parchment, color the circle design with the watercolor pencil. (I made the color darker along the edge of the circle and lighter in the middle.)
5. Working on the back of the parchment on an embossing mat, emboss the floral and critter designs. (Embossed areas will turn white.) Use the spoon embosser to emboss large areas (leaves, flowers).
6. Use the medium embosser for finer details (critters, the centers of the violets, the insides of the lily-of-the-valley flowers).
7. Working on a piece of cardboard from the back of the parchment, stipple the veins of the leaves, using an embossing wheel.
8. Add a simple embossed dot design field for the background, using graph paper as a guide. (Remember all embossing is done on the back over an embossing pad.)
9. Using the one-hole piercer, pierce around or inside the circle. (Remember all piercing is done on the front over a piercing pad.)

Card Assembly:

1. Cut a 3" square window in the pearl paper panel, using a shape cutter and template.
2. Decorate the window panel with corner punches.
3. Tape the parchment crafted panel in the window panel.
4. Tape the framed parchment panel to the front of the folded card.
5. Loop and tie the card tassel around the fold. ❑

Paper Punching

Hole punches have changed dramatically since Benjamin Smith of Massachusetts developed the first paper punch in 1885. (It was a conductor's punch, used for punching train tickets.) Today, European paper crafting artists such as Annelies Karduks of the Netherlands use the decorative punch in dramatic and exciting ways, such as Patchwork Punching. Many paper artists are also punch designers.

Typical hole punches, whether single, multiple, or decorative, have a lever that pushes a bladed cylinder through a sheet of paper. By learning simple punching techniques and using only a few punches, you can create a wide variety of card designs.

Paper Punching Supplies

Punches

A large assortment of punches is available to use for card designs, from simple single-motif hand-held punches to very detailed border punches that punch and emboss as well. For the projects in this book, I used a wide variety of punches from different manufacturers for techniques such as patchwork punching, spirelli, and basic finishing and decorating. If you are unable to locate a specific punch, substitute a similar-size punch with a different design.

Punches: 1) Hand-held punch; 2) Border punch; 3) Circle border punch; 4) Decorative punch; 5) Corner punch; 6) Corner punch with embossing; Punch mat is shown under examples.

Paper Punching Technique

To punch a piece of paper, you need to be able to press the punch with a firm downward motion. I like to stand at a table-height work surface – I find a kitchen counter is generally too high for me. It's a good idea to protect your surface with a thin piece of foam.

Basic Punching, Step by Step:

1. Place the punch on the thin foam on your punching surface.
2. Place the paper in the punch. Before punching, check to be sure you have the paper positioned correctly.
3. Press on the punch in a firm downward motion.

TIPS

• If, after you press the punch, it does not spring back, lightly tap the punch on the foam-covered surface until it does. **Do not** place an object in the punch to push it back.

• For easier punching with detailed punches, lubricate the back of the paper by lightly rubbing it with beeswax.

• A good rule of thumb is the more detailed the punch design, the lighter the paper should be for a good result. Most punches can easily punch through a 60 lb. card paper, and some, like hand-held punches, can punch heavier card weights.

• Take care when using punches – you can damage some of them if you try to force a heavy card weight paper through it.

• For the larger, detailed punches, such as those used for spirelli thread embellishing, you need 60 lb. (or heavier) paper. These large punches can be hard to use – you may need to place the punch on a carpeted floor so you can use your whole weight to punch through the paper.

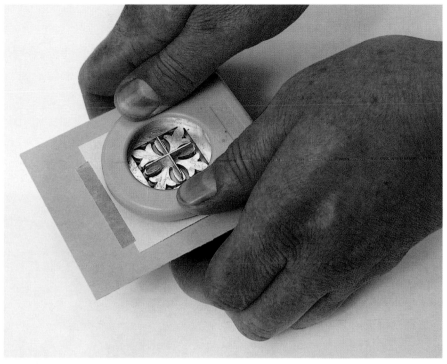

Punching upside down using a paper template.

• You can purchase a power punch that can be used with different punches. It makes using large and detailed punches effortless.

• When using a glue stick to fasten a detailed punched piece of card, use a very gentle touch so you do not get excess glue in the punched-out areas.

Punches That Emboss:

Here's how to use punches that punch as well as emboss a design.

1. Place the paper in the punch. Press down to make the cut.
2. Without moving the paper, push on the punch again with smooth, firm pressure. This action will emboss the motif.

TIP: Card papers show the embossing more than text weight; metallic card paper is best for embossing.

Perfect Placement:

To place a punched motif perfectly on paper, use the punch upside down and with a paper template:

1. Punch a piece of text weight paper to make the template.
2. Using low-tack tape, affix the template to the paper, positioning the punched motif exactly where you want to punch.
3. Place the paper in the punch, aligning the punched template with the punch. Press down to cut.

TIP: Make both a light and a dark template so it will be easy to see the design on all colors of paper.

Patchwork Punched Cards

These little cards show a variety of different designs made with the patchwork punching technique. (The name comes from their resemblance to patchwork quilt designs.) To make them, I used a variety of papers, including rainbow vellum and metallic and solid-color papers.

I used four squares to make each of these cards, but this technique can be adapted for six, eight, or nine squares to make larger cards.

Finished size: 4" square

SUPPLIES

Papers:

Base card – Card weight, solid color, 4" x 8", folded

Front panel – Text weight, metallic or patterned, 3-3/4" square

Punched squares – Text weight, 4" square

Scrap paper (for templates)

Adhesives:

Glue stick

Glue dots (to use with parchment papers)

Embellishments:

Sequin stickers

Threads

Rhinestones

Tools:

Paper trimmer

Punches – 1" design punch, corner punch

Scissors

INSTRUCTIONS

1. Using the paper trimmer, cut four 1-3/4" squares for punching from the text weight paper.
2. Use the 1" punch to cut a positioning template from scrap paper. Use the template to position the punch in the center of each 1-3/4" square piece of paper. Punch the motif.
3. Punch each corner of the paper squares, using the corner punch.
4. Arrange the squares on the front panel, creating the patchwork design. *Options:* On some designs, scissors were used to cut out the central motifs, which were glued in the coordinating-color square. You can also cut away the punched corner pieces and move them around to create interesting effects.
5. Glue arrangement in place.
6. Glue the front panel to the folded card front.
7. Embellish the design with sequin stickers, threads, and/or rhinestones. ❏

Asian Double Fold Card

This card showcases patchwork punching on a larger-size card. The simplicity and spacing of the punched motifs add to the elegant effect.

Finished size: 5" x 6-1/2"

SUPPLIES

Papers:

Card base – Cream card weight, 6-1/2" x 10", folded

Front panels – Metallic gold text weight, 5" x 7", and black and gold origami, 4" x 6"

Inside panels – Black and gold origami, 2" x 6" and metallic gold text weight, 4" x 6"

Punched pieces – Black card weight, 4" x 6"

Panels behind punched pieces – Metallic gold text weight, 4" x 6"

Light color scrap paper (for templates)

Adhesives:

Glue stick

Double-sided tape

Glue dots

Embellishments:

Chinese coin

Gold tassel

Tools:

Shape cutter with circle and square templates

Paper trimmer with cutting and scoring blades

2 Asian-style motif decorative punches, 1"

Ruler

INSTRUCTIONS

1. Measure and mark the card paper on the long side at 2-1/2" and 5" from one end. Score and fold the base card at the marks to create a card with two front panels that open in the middle.

2. Cut two metallic gold text weight panels, each 2-1/4" x 6-1/4". Cut two black and gold origami panels, each 2" x 6". Glue on the front.

3. Cut a piece 2" x 6", from black and gold origami paper. Cut two pieces, each 2" x 6", from metallic gold text weight paper. Glue the two metallic pieces to inside panel, side-by-side with about 1/2" between them at center. Glue the origami paper atop the metallic pieces, centering it.

4. Using the shape cutter and templates, cut three 1-1/2" squares and three 1-1/2" diameter circles for punching from black card paper.

5. Using the shape cutter and templates, cut three 1-1/4" squares and three 1-1/4" diameter circles from metallic gold text weight paper.

6. From scrap paper, make a template for each punch. Using the templates, punch the motifs in the center of the black card pieces. Make three of each motif.

7. Glue a piece of gold metallic paper behind each punched piece. Using the photo as a guide, glue in position on the front panels.

8. Use glue dots to affix the coin to one side in the middle of the card.

9. Loop the gold tassel through the hole in the coin. ❏

Bright Floral Patchwork

Nine squares, arranged like a nine-patch quilt block, are used to make this colorful card. The shaded origami (bokashi) panel creates the optical illusion that the punched squares are different sizes (but they're not). Here, patchwork punching is paired with peel-off stickers.

Finished size: 4-3/4" square

SUPPLIES

Papers:

Card base – White card weight, 4-3/4" x 9-1/2", folded

Front panel – Blue and white shaded origami, 4-1/2" square

Punched pieces – Bright blue card weight, 5" x 1-1/2"

Panels behind punched pieces – Bright pink text weight, 5" x 2"

Scrap paper (for templates)

Adhesives:

Glue stick

Double-sided foam dots, 1/8"

Embellishments:

Peel-off stickers – White and silver floral design, 1" square

Self-adhesive rhinestones – Clear crystal

Tools & Other Supplies:

Paper trimmer with cutting and scoring blades

Punches – 1" circular flower, 1/2" daisy

Gel pens – Variety of bright colors

Pink chalk and applicator

INSTRUCTIONS

1. Glue the shaded origami panel on the front of the card.
2. With the shape cutter and templates, cut out five 1-1/2" squares for punching from bright blue card paper.
3. Use the 1" flower punch to punch a paper template from scrap paper. Using the template for positioning, punch a flower in the center of the bright blue card squares.
4. Cut five 1" squares of bright pink text paper. Position one on the back of each punched piece. Glue in place.

5. Using pink chalk, color the petals of the punched flowers.
6. Punch five small daisies from the pink paper. Affix a rhinestone in the center of each pink daisy. Attach a daisy at the center of each punched panel with a double-sided foam dot.
7. Glue the finished punched panels to the front panel of the card, using the photo as a guide.
8. Apply four peel-off stickers to the front of the card as shown in the photo. Color the stickers with gel pens. ❏

The Fold-and-Punch Technique

Simply folding, then punching origami paper pieces creates this effect. Use only lighter-weight origami paper and punches with simple designs. (Punches with detailed designs won't work on multiple layers of paper.) Solid-color and shaded origami papers – folded to make a maximum of four layers – give the best results. Experiment with different types of folds to create different designs.

Fold-and-Punch, Step by Step:

1. Cut a 3" square piece of bokashi (shaded) origami paper.
2. Fold in half, then in half again to form a 1-1/2" square.
3. Punch the folded square. You can use part or all of the punch motif. If the design is punched crooked, don't worry – when unfolded it will (magically!) become an attractive pattern.
4. Glue the punched design on backing paper, using a glue stick. Here, the same-color bokashi paper creates a beautiful effect.

Folding and punching steps:
Left: Shaded origami paper cut in a square.
Top center: Folded paper.

Right: The unfolded design glued onto backing paper.
Bottom center: Folded piece has been punched.

FOLDED &
PUNCHED CARDS

Instructions on page 104

Punched Medallions Technique

You can make wonderful medallion designs using corner punches on folded paper. Three-in-one corner punches are great for these – you can create a variety of designs with one punch.

Punched Medallions, Step by Step:
1. Cut a 2" square of thin origami paper.
2. Fold in half, then in half again to form a 1" square.
3. Punch all four corners with a corner punch. Unfold to reveal the medallion. ❑

Punched medallion design steps:
Left: Shaded origami paper cut in a square.
Top center: Folded paper.
Bottom center: Folded piece has been punched.
Right: The unfolded design.

Folded & Punched Cards

Pictured on pages 103 and 105

These small gift cards are made using the fold-and-punch technique and are accented with peel-off stickers. Using different types of origami paper, punches, and stickers creates a variety of looks.

Finished size: 3-1/2" square

SUPPLIES

Papers:

Base card – Solid color card weight, 3-1/2 " x 7", folded

Front panel – Metallic or solid colored origami, 3-1/4" square

Folded-and-punched panel – Bokashi (shaded) origami, 3" x 3"

Backing panel – Bokashi (shaded) origami

Adhesives:

Glue stick

Embellishments:

Peel-off stickers – Motifs, borders

Sequin stickers

Tools & Other Supplies:

Punches – Mosaic or other design, 1"

Scissors

Gel pens – Variety of bright colors

BASIC INSTRUCTIONS

1. Using the fold-and-punch technique described at the beginning of this section, fold and punch the 3" square origami paper piece.
2. Unfold the paper. Glue on the backing panel.
3. *Option:* Add peel-off stickers directly to the punched panel.
4. Glue the punched panel to the front panel.
5. Glue the front panel to the folded card front.
6. *Option:* Add peel-off border stickers to embellish or frame the design.

Tapa Cards Technique

These cards resemble tapa, a type of cloth produced throughout the South Pacific. The people of Tonga, Tahiti, Fiji, Samoa, and other islands make bark cloth in distinctive styles for functional and ceremonial purposes. The often elaborate patterns are applied by block printing or by dipping leaves in dye and pressing them on the cloth. The patterns represent various aspects of their lives and are usually black with shades of rust and brown. The combination of fold-and-punch techniques and Mola cutting give these cards a tropical look like that of tapa fabrics. See page 22 for step-by-step Mola Cutting instructions.

The Tapa Technique, Step by Step;
1. Cut a 3-1/2" square of natural-color origami paper.
2. Fold in half, then in half again to make a square.
3. Punch the design. Unfold.
4. Glue the punched piece to the front panel.
5. Working one layer at a time, tape a layer of origami paper to the back and cut out the design, using the Mola Cutting technique.
6. Using the same punch, punch a motif from a scrap of one of the Mola-cut layers. Glue at the center of the punched panel.
7. Tape the finished panel on the card front, using double-sided tape. Add embellishments as desired. ❏

Tapa Cards

Finished size: 4" square

SUPPLIES

Papers:

Base card – Dark brown or black card weight, 4" x 8", folded

Front panel – Coordinated dark hue card weight, 3-3/4" square

Folded-and-punched panel – Natural-color origami, 3-1/2" square

Layers for Mola cutting – Solid, patterned, and metallic origami, 3-1/2" squares

Adhesives:

Glue stick

Double-sided tape

Embellishments:

Copper brads

Decorative fibers

Tools:

Punch – Mosaic or other motif, 1"

Art knife

Cutting mat

INSTRUCTIONS

1. Following the fold-and-punch technique, fold and punch the natural-color origami paper.
2. Unfold the design. Glue to the front panel paper piece.
3. Working one layer at a time, tape origami paper on the back and cut, using the Mola Cutting technique. Use the project photos for design and cutting ideas.
4. Punch a motif from one of the under-layer papers. Glue it to the center of the punched panel.
5. Tape the finished panel to the card front using double-sided tape.
6. Embellish with copper brads and decorative fibers. ❏

THE INTRUDER

Spirelli Thread Embellishing

Spirelli or string art cards are embellished with thread. I have used the traditional techniques of winding thread around notched shapes and embroidering thread on punched shapes. (The embroidery technique is sometimes called curve stitching.)

The unique feature of these geometric thread designs is that each pattern is a set of points located evenly on a shape. The points are then connected with straight thread lines in a numerical sequence, creating curves. (The idea can be used to show children how curved patterns can be made with straight lines.) Patterns created with string art can be highly complex or simple connect-the-dot type patterns. String art, popular in the 1960s and 70s, is made by winding colored string around a grid of nails hammered into a fabric-covered wooden board.

Spirelli thread embellishing, a European string art technique that has caught on in North America, has been adapted for use in card making and scrapbooking. The technique involves wrapping decorative thread around a notched paper shape to create a geometric design. (It reminds me of a toy called a Spirograph that I played with in the 70s that, when rolled, created designs on paper. Spirelli is also the name of a spiral-shaped pasta.)

Thread Embellishing Supplies

In previous sections, you've seen how decorative fibers of various types can add whimsy, dimension, and color to cards. Packages of fibers and ready-made card tassels, which add a finishing touch to cards, can be found in paper crafting stores.

For the spirelli thread wrapping and paper embroidery techniques in this section, threads are used for card decorating. I prefer fine rayon threads (the kind used for machine embroidery); the fine metallic threads made for hand and machine embroidery also can be used. If you want a more substantial thread, silk embroidery floss or ordinary two- or three-strand cotton embroidery floss works well.

Spirelli materials: 1) Spirelli punches; 2) Shapes cut with decorative scissors; 3) Needles: 4) Thread;
5) Pre-punched spirelli shapes

Spirelli Thread Technique

Photo 1 – Threading the notched shape to create a spirelli design.

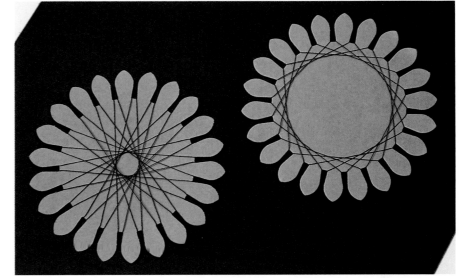

Photo 2 – Design at left shows a few spaces between the threads. The design at right with many spaces between the threads.

Spirelli Thread Wrapping, Step by Step:

1. Start with a notched symmetrical paper shape – you can use pre-cut spirelli shapes, a shape made with a spirelli punch, or a shape cut with decorative scissors.

   If you're using a pre-cut shape, move on to step 2.

   If you're using a spirelli punch, follow the step-by-step instructions for punching found earlier in this book and use a light card-weight paper (about a 60-lb.) TIP: Place the punch on the floor to get enough force to punch through the card paper.

Continued on next page

Photo 3 – Embellished and layered spirelli designs.

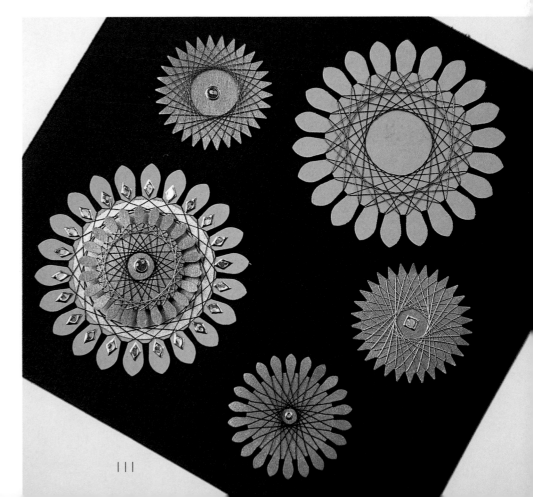

Spirelli Thread Technique, continued from page 111

To make a notched shape with decorative scissors, trace around a shape template on the back of a piece of card paper. Cut out the notched shape with decorative edge scissors (pinking, stamp edge, corkscrew, scallop).

2. Tape the end of the thread to the back of the notched shape.

3. Bring the thread to the front between two notched points and around the back again.

4. Continue the design by bringing the thread to the front around the next notch on the shape, pull across the front and to the notch beside the previous threaded notch. Continue to wrap the thread around the shape until you reach the starting point. Tape the thread end to the back with tape and trim. The number of notches between the wrapped points determines the finished design. The fewer the notches, the larger the center design and vice versa.

5. You can layer the threads on the notched shape and layer finished shapes with foam tape. Sequin stickers and rhinestones work especially well as embellishments.

Dimensional Spirelli Cards

SUPPLIES

Papers:

Card base – Metallic or solid-color card weight, 3-3/4" x 7-1/2", folded

Front panel, punched shapes – Metallic or solid-color card weight

Scrap paper (for template)

Adhesives:

Transparent tape

Double-sided tape

Double-sided foam tape

Embellishments:

Metallic threads to match paper colors

Crystal rhinestone

Tools:

Spirelli punches – Splash punch, 2-3/4" diameter; classic punch, 1-1/4" diameter

Scissors

These elegant cards use a large and a small spirelli punch to make the notched shapes. Both the positive and negative punched shapes are used to create a dimensional design using the spirelli thread wrapping technique. The different cards are made using the same techniques with different colors of papers and threads.

Finished size: 3-3/4" square

INSTRUCTIONS

1. Punch a template from scrap paper, using the large punch. Use the template as a guide to punch the large notched shape in the middle of the front panel paper. Reserve the punched-out piece.

2. Punch the small notched shape from the same card paper, using the small punch.

3. Following the step-by-step instructions for the Spirelli Thread Wrapping Technique, wrap each notched shape with two colors of thread.

4. Mount the punched paper panel on the card base with double-sided tape.

5. Mount the large spirelli shape on the punched shape with foam tape, rotating the spirelli shape slightly to create the starburst design.

6. Mount the small wrapped spirelli shape at the center of the large shape, using foam tape.

7. Place a rhinestone in the center of the small shape. ❑

Three Spirelli Card Designs

These three cards are made using pre-cut notched shapes that are available in card shops. (You can substitute card paper cut with scallop-edge decorative scissors if you can't locate pre-cut shapes.) On all the cards, the notched shapes are shaded with a stamp pad and stencil brush.

Spirelli Travel Card

Finished size: 4-1/2" x 5"

SUPPLIES

Papers:
Base card – Dark brown pearl card weight, 4-1/2" x 10", folded
Notched shape – Cream card weight pre-cut shape, 3-1/2" square

Adhesives:
Transparent tape
Double-sided foam tape

Embellishments:
Embroidery thread – Copper metallic
Peel-off stickers, travel theme – Copper
Gel pens – Black, red

Tools & Other Supplies:
Scissors
Stamp pad – Sepia brown
Stencil brush
Walnut ink liquid spray

INSTRUCTIONS

1. Using the stamp pad and stencil brush, shade the edges of the notched shape.
2. Spray the card lightly with walnut ink to create the appearance of an old map.
3. Wrap the notched shape with copper thread, Following the instructions for the Spirelli Thread Wrapping Technique.
4. Affix a variety of copper peel-off stickers to the front of the base card.
5. Affix a compass sticker to the front of the spirelli paper piece.
6. Color the peel-off stickers with gel pens.
7. Mount the spirelli piece on the card front with the foam tape. ❏

Spirelli Renaissance Card

Finished size: 3-3/4" square

SUPPLIES

Papers:
Base card – Dark brown pearl card weight, 3-3/4" x 7-1/2", folded
Notched shape – Cream card weight pre-cut shape, 3-1/2" square

Adhesives:
Transparent tape
Double-sided foam tape
Glue dot

Embellishments:
Embroidery thread – Gold metallic
Peel-off stickers – Gold border
Flattened bottle cap and sticker

Tools & Other Supplies:
Scissors
Stamp pad – Sepia brown
Stencil brush
Rubber stamp – Renaissance theme

INSTRUCTIONS

1. Using the stamp pad and stencil brush, shade the edges of the notched shape.
2. Stamp the shape with the stamp and sepia ink.
3. Wrap the notched shape with the gold thread, following the Spirelli Thread Wrapping Technique.
4. Affix a gold sticker border to the front of the base card.
5. Mount the spirelli piece on the front of the card with double-sided tape.
6. Glue the bottle cap embellishment in place with a glue dot. ❏

Spirelli Floral Tag instructions begin on page 116.

Spirelli Floral Tag

Pictured on page 115

Finished size: 3" x 4-1/2"

SUPPLIES

Papers:

Base card – Light purple card weight, 4" x 6"

Backing panels – Light blue and light blue pearl card weight, 4" x 6"

Notched shape: Light purple pre-cut shape, 3" triangle

Adhesives:

Transparent tape, Double-sided tape, Double-sided foam tape

Embellishments:

Embroidery thread – Silver metallic

Stickers – Silver sequins, dimensional floral

Peel-off sticker – Silver "Congratulations"

Eyelet, Decorative fibers

Tools & Other Supplies:

Shape cutter with tag template

Decorative scissors – Scallop edge

Scissors, Stencil brush, Eyelet setting tool

Stamp pad – Purple

INSTRUCTIONS

1. Using the shape cutter and tag template, cut 4-1/2" tags from light blue and light purple card papers.
2. Tape the light purple tag shape to the light blue pearl paper. Following the shape, cut out a larger tag from the pearl paper, using scallop-edge scissors.
3. Randomly wrap the scalloped tag shape with silver thread.
4. Tape the light blue tag on the back of the thread-wrapped tag to cover the threads and tape.
5. Using the stamp pad and stencil brush, shade the edges of the triangular notched shape. Let dry.
6. Add sequin stickers to the edges.
7. Wrap the notched shape with silver thread, following the instructions for the Spirelli Thread Wrapping Technique.
8. Add the "Congratulations" sticker at the bottom on the front.
9. Mount the spirelli piece on the tag front with foam tape.
10. Set the eyelet at the top.
11. Thread decorative fibers through the eyelet. ❏

Galaxy Card

Pictured at right

Finished size: 5-1/2" x 4-1/4"

SUPPLIES

Papers:

Card base – Black card weight, 5-1/2" x 8-1/2", folded

Front panel – Black pearl card weight, 5-1/4" x 4"

Notched shapes – Black pearl card weight

Adhesives:

Transparent tape

Double-sided tape

Double-sided foam tape

Embellishments:

Threads – Silver metallic, dark blue metallic, black metallic

Sequin stickers – Gold

Tools:

Decorative scissors – Pinking. mini pinking

Templates – Oval, circle

INSTRUCTIONS

1. Trace a variety of circle and oval shapes, 1" to 2", on black pearl paper.
2. Cut out the shapes with pinking scissors.
3. Wrap the threads around the notched shapes, following the instructions for the Spirelli Thread Wrapping Technique. Double and triple wrap some of the shapes for variety.
4. Tape the front panel to the front of the base card.
5. Mount the spirelli shapes to the front of the card, using both the regular and foam double-sided tape. Layer one shape by taping a small spirelli shape on a large one.
6. Affix sequin stickers to the centers of the spirelli shapes and to the card front to complete your galaxy. ❏

Cards with Clustered Spirelli Shapes

Clusters of spirelli shapes on dark colored card paper were used for both of these cards. The notched shapes were cut out with pinking scissors from the same color card papers as the front panels so the spirelli thread designs really stand out.

Fireworks Card

Finished size: 5-3/4" x 4-3/4"

SUPPLIES

Papers:

Card base – Blue pearl card weight, 5-3/4" x 9-1/2", folded

Front panel – Black card weight, 5-1/2" x 4-1/2"

Notched shapes – Black card weight

Adhesives:

Transparent tape

Double-sided tape

Double-sided foam tape

Embellishments:

Threads – Silver metallic, colored metallic

Colored rhinestones

Silver gel pen

Tools:

Decorative scissors – Pinking

Templates – Oval, circle

INSTRUCTIONS

1. Trace a variety of circle and oval shapes, 1" to 2", on black card paper.
2. Cut out the shapes with pinking scissors.
3. Wrap the threads around the notched shapes, following the instructions for the Spirelli Thread Wrapping Technique. Double wrap some of the shapes for variety.

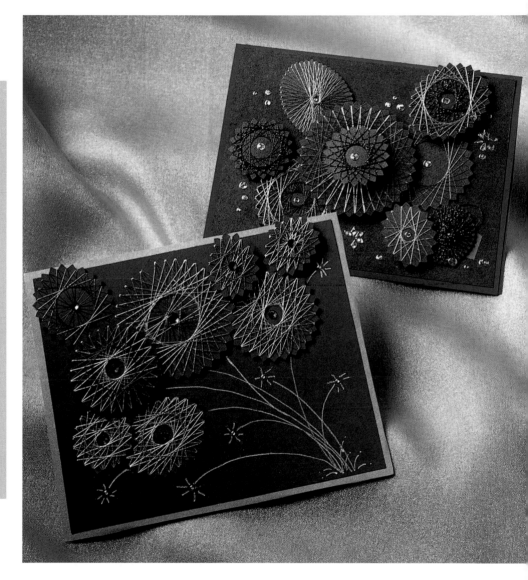

4. Tape the front panel to the front of the base card.
5. Mount the spirelli shapes to the front of the card, using the photo as a guide, with both regular and foam double-sided tape. Overlap the shapes slightly to form the design.
6. Affix the colored rhinestones to the centers of the spirelli shapes and on the card front.
7. Add the silver lines and accents with the gel pen. ❑

SUPPLIES

Papers:

Card base: Bright pink card weight, 6" x 11"

Notched shapes – Bright yellow, green, orange, and pink card weight

Adhesives:

Transparent tape, Double-sided tape

Embellishments:

Threads – Gold metallic, colored

Stickers – Colored rhinestones, rhinestone alphabet

Tools:

Decorative scissors – Pinking

Square template

Paper trimmer with cutting and scoring blades

Peace-Joy-Love Card

Square thread-wrapped shapes in bright colors decorate an accordion-folded card. Rhinestone alphabet stickers spell out PEACE, JOY, and LOVE.

Finished size: 4-1/2" x 6"

INSTRUCTIONS

1. Using the paper trimmer with the scoring blade, score the base card paper at 2-1/2", 3-3/4", 6", and 8". Fold along the scored lines to create an accordion-folded base card.
2. Trace a variety of square shapes, 1", 1-1/4" and 1-1/2", on the various colors of card stock paper.
3. Cut out the shapes with pinking scissors. Layer the squares to create a total of seven single- and multi-layered notched shapes.
4. Wrap the threads around the notched shapes, following the instructions for the Spirelli Thread Wrapping Technique.
5. Using the photo as a guide for placement, tape the spirelli shapes to the card between the folds.
6. Add rhinestone stickers to the centers of the spirelli shapes.
7. Spell out "Peace," "Love," and "Joy" with rhinestone letter stickers. ❑

SUPPLIES

Papers:

Card base – Dark maroon card weight, 6" x 11"

Notched shapes – Burnt orange, sage green, pink card weight

Adhesives:

Glue stick, Transparent tape, Double-sided tape

Embellishments:

Threads – Gold metallic, colored

Tools:

Spirelli punches – Large flower, small flower

Shape cutter with circle template

Paper trimmer with cutting and scoring blades

Spirelli Circles Card

A variety of colorful circular shapes, cut with spirelli punches and a shape cutter with a circle template, decorate this dark-colored accordion-folded card.

Finished size: 4-1/2" x 6"

INSTRUCTIONS

1. Using the paper trimmer with the scoring blade, score the base card paper at 2-1/2", 3-3/4", 6", and 8". Fold along the scored lines to create an accordion-folded base card.
2. Punch a variety of flower shapes from the various colors of card stock paper.
3. Using the shape cutter and circle template, cut a variety of circles from the various colored card papers.
4. With the glue stick, glue circles of different colors on the notched shapes, layering some of the circles. See the project photo for placement ideas.
5. Wrap the threads around the notched shapes, following instructions for the Spirelli Thread Wrapping Technique.
6. Using the photo as a guide, tape the spirelli and circle shapes to the card between the folds. ❑

Instructions for Bright Happy Birthday Card begin on page 120.

SUPPLIES

Papers:

Card base: Black card weight,
7" x 10"

Metallic panel, 2-1/4" x 6-1/2"

Notched shapes – Bright yellow,
orange, pink, and black card
weight

Adhesives:

Transparent tape, Double-sided tape

Embellishments:

Decorative Yarn

Stickers – peel-off "Happy Birthday"

Tools:

Decorative scissors – Pinking

Square template, Embossing heat
tool

Paper trimmer with cutting and
scoring blades

Bright Happy Birthday Card

Pictured on page 119

Three square shapes with pinked edges are wrapped with spirelli-style
threads for a triple-happy birthday.

Finished size: 7" x 5-1/2"

INSTRUCTIONS

1. Cut edges of base card with pinking scissors. Fold the base card in half and
   score.
2. Trace a 2" square shape onto each of the pink, yellow and orange card stock
   pieces. Trace three 2" squares onto the black card stock.
3. Cut out the shapes with pinking scissors. Cut the black squares slightly outside of your traced lines; cut the colored squares slightly inside of your
   traced lines.
4. Wrap the threads around the three colored notched shapes, following the
   instructions for the Spirelli Thread Wrapping Technique.
5. Layer the colored squares on top of black squares, securing with double-
   sided tape.
6. Tape the spirelli squares to the metallic panel using double-sided tape.
7. Tape the Metallic panel to the card front.
8. Attach the "Happy Birthday" stickers on card front below metallic panel.
9. Add yarn at top fold of card. ❑

SUPPLIES

Papers:

Card base – Soft green pearl card
weight, 9" x 6-1/2", folded

Notched shapes – Light purple pearl
card weight

Adhesives:

Transparent tape

Double-sided tape

Glue stick

Embellishments:

Threads – Gold metallic

Laser-cut mini daisies (or a mini
daisy punch)

Stickers – Sequins

Tools:

Templates – Square, rectangle

Decorative scissors – Pinking

Squares & Daisies Card

Pictured at right

Finished card size: 4-1/2" x 6-1/2"

INSTRUCTIONS

1. Using the templates, trace:
   One 3-3/4" x 2-1/2" rectangle
   Two 2-1/2" x 1-1/2" rectangles
   One 1-1/2" square
   One 2-1/2" square.
   Cut around the shapes with pinking scissors to make the notches.
2. Wrap gold thread around the notched shapes, following the instructions for
   the Spirelli Thread Wrapping Technique.
3. Tape the thread-wrapped shapes to the card front, using the photo as a
   guide for placement.
4. Use a glue stick to affix the daisies to the front of the card, and to the
   centers of the thread-wrapped shapes.
5. Add a sequin sticker to the center of each daisy. ❑

Pictured at right: Dragonfly Card and Daisy Card. Instructions begin on page 122.

Happy Birthday

SUPPLIES

Papers:

Card base – White card weight, 8-1/2" x 7-1/2", folded

Front panel – Bright blue card weight, 4-1/4" x 7-1/2"

Notched shapes – White, yellow, and green card weight

Adhesives:

Transparent tape, Double-sided tape

Double-sided foam dots, Paper glue

Embellishments:

Threads – Gold metallic, silver metallic, green

Daisy buttons, shanks removed

Tools:

Spirelli punches – Small classic shape

Shape cutter with flower and leaf templates

Decorative scissors – Pinking

Daisy Card

Pictured on page 121

Finished size: 4-1/4" x 7-1/2"

INSTRUCTIONS

1. Cut the edge of the bright blue front panel piece with pinking scissors to make a notched panel.
2. Wrap the notched panel with silver metallic thread.
3. With the shape cutter and flower template, cut four daisy shapes from white card. Tape the blossoms together to make a layered daisy.
4. With the spirelli punch, punch two notched shapes from the yellow paper for the daisy centers.
5. Using the flower template, trace two leaf shapes on green card paper. Cut around the shapes with pinking scissors.
6. Wrap the threads around the notched leaf and flower shapes, following the instructions for the Spirelli Thread Wrapping Technique. Use gold thread on the white flower petals and yellow centers and green thread on the leaves.
7. Use foam dots to mount the yellow centers on the white flower petals.
8. Tape the thread-embellished leaves and flower shapes to the card, using the photo as a guide for placement.
9. Glue a daisy button at the center of each flower. ❑

SUPPLIES

Papers:

Card base – Lime green card weight, 5-3/4 " x 9-1/2", folded

Front panel – Purple card weight, 4-1/2" x 5-1/2"

Notched shapes – Bright blue and green card weight

Adhesives:

Transparent tape, Double-sided tape, Double-sided foam dots

Embellishments:

Threads – Gold metallic, silver metallic

Stickers – Sequins, peel-off "Happy Birthday"

Decorative fibers yarn, Gold dragonfly charm

Tools:

Circle template, Ellipse template

Decorative scissors – Stamp edge

Hand-held hole punch, 1/4"

Dragonfly Card

Pictured on page 121

Finished size: 4-3/4" x 5-3/4"

INSTRUCTIONS

1. For the wings, cut two each of the following ellipse sizes from blue card stock, using stamp edge scissors to create the notches – 2", 1-3/4", 1-1/2".
2. For the body cut the following from the green card stock using the circle templates – one 1" circle, three 3/4" circles. Use the stamp edge scissors to cut.
3. For wings, wrap threads around the notched shapes, following the instructions for the Spirelli Thread Wrapping Technique. Use silver thread to wrap end-to-end for the wings, then gold thread for the curved design.
4. Wrap the threads around the green shapes, following the spirelli technique.
5. Punch two circles from green paper for the eyes, using the hand-held punch.
6. Use foam dots to mount the green thread-wrapped shapes for the dragonfly's body and the green circles for the eyes. Use double-sided tape to attach the thread-wrapped wings. Use the photo as a guide for placement.
7. Accent the dragonfly with the sequin stickers. Add the "Happy Birthday" sticker.
8. Tie decorative fibers yarn around the fold of the card and add the gold charm at the knots. ❑

Spirelli Embroidery Technique

You can also add spirelli-type designs to cards using a needle and thread. Simply use spirelli punches to create the shapes or trace and cut shapes with decorative scissors, then make stitching holes with a piercing tool and run thread through the holes. Since the thread is not wrapped around the punched or cut paper pieces, you can use any weight paper, including bokashi (shaded) origami paper, which yields spectacular effects.

Spirelli Embroidery, Step by Step:

1. Punch the spirelli shape from bokashi origami paper.
2. Glue the shape on a card paper piece.
3. Using a one-hole piercer, make the holes for the thread along the edge of the punched shape. *Option:* Pierce other notches or points of the design to create different patterns.

Spirelli embroidery technique.

4. Thread a needle. Tape the thread to the back of the card and bring the needle up through a pierced hole. Sew the spirelli-style design, using the pierced holes as a guide for placing the thread. ❏

Pictured at left: Red & Purple Card. Instructions begin on page 124.

Red & Purple Card

Pictured on page 123

Finished size: 5-1/4" square

SUPPLIES

Papers:

Base card – Dusty purple card weight, 5-1/4" x 10-1/2", folded

Backing panel – Dusty purple card weight, 5" square

Insert for windows – Red pearl card weight, 4-1/2" square; black card weight, 4-1/2" square

Spirelli shape – Red/purple shaded origami paper, 3" square

Adhesives:

Glue stick

Transparent tape

Double-sided tape

Embellishments:

Threads – Gold metallic, purple metallic

Purple rhinestone

Tools:

Spirelli punch – Large splash shape

Shape cutter with circle template

One-hole piercing tool

Sewing needle

Small punch – Sun motif

INSTRUCTIONS

1. Punch the spirelli shape from shaded origami paper. Glue the shape on the red pearl paper piece.
2. Using the one-hole piercer, make holes for the thread, using the spirelli shape as a guide.
3. Thread a needle with purple thread. Using the pierced holes, stitch the inner design, following the step-by-step spirelli embroidery instructions. Stitch the outer design with gold thread.
4. Cut a round window, 3-1/2" diameter, in the front of the dusty purple base card.
5. Cut a round window, 3" diameter, in black card paper.
6. Mount the black paper piece and red pearl paper piece behind the round window on the card front. Center the embroidered motif.
7. Tape the backing panel inside of the card behind the window.
8. Punch a sun shape from black paper. Glue at the center of the thread-wrapped motif. Glue the rhinestone in the center. ❑

Birthday Wishes Card

Pictured at right

SUPPLIES

Papers:

Base card – 3-1/2" x 7" light green card weight

Front panel – 3-1/2" square medium green card weight

White parchment paper

White copy paper

Adhesives:

Double-sided tape

Low-tack masking tape

Embellishments:

Thread – Gold

1/8" bronze metal brad

Tools:

Piercing tool

Scissors

Needle

Piercing mat

INSTRUCTIONS

1. Fold card in half and score.
2. Trim medium green panel so that it is slightly smaller than 3-1/2". Tape medium green panel to front of card.
3. Cut leaves and circles from parchment according to patterns.
4. Temporarily tape these parchment pieces in place while using the gold thread to stitch according to photo.
5. Place card on piercing matt and use piercing tool to add a decorative border around edge of card.
6. With a computer or a rubber stamp, make "Birthday Wishes" sentiment on white copy paper, approximately 1-1/2" x 1/2". Attach sentiment to card with brad. ❑

See pattern on page 127.

Also pictured at right: Sunburst Card and Best Wishes Card. Instructions begin on page 126.